'*Studentdom* is the essential g[...]
gating their way through un[...]
    Matt Bird,

'Matt gives an excellent and integrated guide to life as a student. He accurately describes many of the challenges that Christians stepping into the world of studentdom are likely to face. I am really pleased to see a book which takes such a holistic and practical approach. This book will equip and guide you as you start university and prepare to transition into the world of work. I thoroughly recommend it.'

    Louise Donkin, SPEAK Network Founding Co-ordinator

'*Studentdom* gives a first-class insight into student life and would be a real help to anyone thinking about or preparing to go to university. *Studentdom* is both perceptive and comprehensive in its coverage of the issues that students face before, during and after university. I have not come across another book like *Studentdom* and it should be essential reading for sixth-form students before they apply to university, and then kept close at hand all the way through to graduation.'

    Gez Perry, Navigator Student Representative

'I've got a 17-year-old daughter considering university. As soon as I'd finished reading *Studentdom* I gave it to her. It cuts to the quick of the key issues facing a student who wants to get it right as a Christian, but has a lightness of touch that makes it so easy to read. Great stuff!'

    Graham Daniels, General Director, Christians In Sport

'Matt's book is a wide-ranging and immensely practical drive-by tour guide of student life. He hits all the key sights and steers over the major road blocks helping us to get ready for the ultimate road trip.'

Andy Atkins, Agape

'Matt has combined godly wisdom, practical experience and passion for Jesus in this excellent book. His love for students and a desire to see them thrive and be Christ-like in the student world shines through. Any Christian student who engages with Matt's biblical and practical ideas will be thoroughly equipped for the challenges that lie ahead. I shall warmly commend it to every student that I know.'

Andrew Morsley, Student Worker, The Steward's Trust

'Student culture is not what it used to be and Matt does well to unpack some of these changes so that Christian students can go with their eyes open to the pitfalls and opportunities. This practical, down-to-earth message will be a useful insight into student life for all wannabe students. Matt Stuart's book will provide a very timely resource.'

Rich Wilson, Network Manager, Fusion
– The Student Cell Movement

'With *Studentdom* Matt Stuart has provided a greatly needed resource for young Christians starting at university. The book is packed full of good advice based on Matt's own student experience, backed up by sound biblical truths. This book should be compulsory reading for all young Christians planning to go to university. I wish I'd read it before I started!'

Simon Lucas, University of Essex Christian Union Committee 2000–2001

'A must-read for anyone heading off to university. This book skillfully takes you step by step through the trials and tribulations of student life, in a down to earth and humourous way. A top manual to have as a Christian living in studentdom, I would recommend it to anyone . . . just wish it had been around a few years earlier for me.'

Sara Garvie, University of Leeds

'The university years present many challenges. *Studentdom* offers a very practical approach for every Christian as they embark on this significant phase of their life.'

Lizi Jackson, Director, Alpha for Students

'As parents of four children we found this book of helpful information. It helps unravel the process of higher education in a clear, concise and easy to read manner. We believe it is a valuable resource for students and their parents and that those who have read it will not only be better informed about the system but also able to tackle potential problems before they arise. We wish this book had been published before our first child reached this stage in their life.'

Richard and Anne Firth, parents

studentdom

**MATT
STUART**

survivor

ISBN 1 84291 079 5

Published by
KINGSWAY COMMUNICATIONS LTD
Lottbridge Drove, Eastbourne BN23 6NT, England.
Email: books@kingsway.co.uk

Book design and production for the publishers by
Bookprint Creative Services, P.O. Box 827, BN21 3YJ, England.
Printed in Great Britain.

contents

thanks

To my wife, Claire, our family and friends for their love and support.

To Matt Bird for his investment in my life, and the rest of the Joshua Generation team – Row Bazlinton, Mark Dinsdale, Adam Eakins, Mary Johnson and Steve Spriggs – for their amazing belief and encouragement.

To Jonathan Balding, Roger Bretherton, Rachel Fenning, Anne Firth, David Hawes, Tim Hughes, Lizzie Jenkins, Gary Kennaugh, David Lindsell, Mark Lloyd Davies, Simon Lucas, Pete McKnight, Sophie Parker, John Risbridger, Richard Shorter, Row Shuttleworth, Phil Simcock, Jenny Spriggs, Rie Taylor, and Rich Wilson for reading parts of the manuscript and helping me to shape this book.

To all my student friends, who continue to inspire and encourage me.

To Dave Roberts, Richard Herkes, Les Moir and Carolyn Owen at Kingsway for their belief in me, their help and advice.

And most of all: to Jesus, who has always given me more than I deserve.

foreword

The student years can be the best years of your life (they were for me), or they can be a nightmare. Certainly those years help to form us as people more than anything else. I have to say, for myself, they formed me more than informed me!

I have long wished for a book to help prepare us for the radical changes and unique opportunities that come with student life. Well at last, here it is. This is a great book and will prove an indispensable resource for those beginning the journey. Matt does not speak from an ivory tower. It is not that long since he was a student and, ever since, he has devoted himself to working within and reflecting upon the student scene. This book is the fruit of all that.

Studentdom has everything. It is intensely practical, giving the low-down on all aspects of student life from freshers week onwards. It is honest about the challenges and opportunities and addresses all the issues in a forth-right way.

The book is also great applied theology. Matt has clearly thought through the issues biblically and I have been helped by his insights. Matt's conviction (and mine for that matter) is that there has to be a third way for the follower of Jesus between the two common extremes. One of those is to retreat into the Christian parallel universe where we may think it is safe and won't be contaminated by engaging with the world – but also where we are useless. The other extreme is an unreflective headlong rush to 'be relevant' that results in there being nothing distinctive about us. The third way is the difficult but ultimately very rewarding process of thinking and praying through the issues biblically and working out before God the areas where we need to make a stand. Matt's analogy here to the life of Daniel as a student away from home is particularly helpful.

Studentdom is thought-through, practically helpful and, like its author, has integrity. I warmly commend it to you.

Mike Pilavachi
April 2002

introduction

Student culture

I love to travel. Nothing beats going somewhere you have never been before and experiencing things that are new to you. I remember when my friend (also called Matt) and I were travelling to Australia to go to a conference in Sydney. We decided to go on the cheapest flight we could find, no matter what the airline was or where it stopped. Having searched high and low we managed to find a bargain on a Gulf Air flight that fitted in perfectly with the timetable of our trip. When the day of our departure came, we dressed smartly, hoping for an upgrade on the plane, and met up at Heathrow, excited about our trip together. We didn't get our upgrade but instead set off cramped into the economy cabin.

Neither Matt nor I are very good at sitting around for

very long and this flight turned out to be a bit of a nightmare. Once we had watched a couple of movies and read the in-flight magazine we were bored out of our minds. To make matters worse the airline company seemed to have forgotten that we were flying to the other side of the world and had decided to operate some sort of bus service. Our flight stopped everywhere, dropping people off and picking others up more regularly than the number 79 that stops at the end of my road. It was ridiculous.

Things did liven up a bit when Matt managed to spill half a pint of orange juice down his trousers and spent the next three hours wandering round the plane in his boxer shorts, trying to persuade the air stewardess to dry his soaked chinos with a hairdryer. Thirty hours and several stops later, we touched down in Oz, desperate to get off the plane and see some of this place we had heard so much about.

Our twelve days in Australia were fantastic. It is an awesome country, full of new experiences, yet strangely reminiscent of things familiar. Take the Blue Mountains, for example. This is one of the most beautiful places in the world, and visiting here is a must if you are in South East Australia. Yet it's a place where I felt comfortable and at ease. Walking around Sydney is no different. Amazing structures such as the Opera House and Harbour Bridge were all around us but, with the help of a map, within a few hours we felt right at home. In many ways the familiarity of our culture at home had prepared us well for the new culture we would find in a country the other side of the world.

Much like the British visitor to Australia, studentdom is a different world, yet one that is strangely familiar. There are some elements of what is perceived as student culture that have become legendary. Drinking, drugs, sex, late nights and later mornings, a diet of toast and beans, debt, sport and travel; they are all covered in this book, but none of them is what student culture is about. They are signs that point towards this culture – stories that tell us what it looks like, but they are not it. In many cases they are stereotypes that cannot hope to describe the complex multiplicity that is student culture.

So these are not the things this introduction will focus on, because to define student culture by way of one or two superficial characteristics would hardly scratch the surface. Broader themes that overarch the whole of student life give much more scope for the discerning Christian student to bring truth to their friends. Trying to tell someone that they should not have sex with their partner because they are not married is virtually pointless. Explaining that community is such a valuable commodity in student culture because God made us for relationship with him and one another is a much more effective approach. What then are these wider themes that encapsulate student life and speak of its culture? I have mentioned one already, so we shall start there.

Community

'Friendship' and 'community' are two words that students rarely speak but know a lot about. As you go to university you should expect it to be a very friendly place. Student life is geared to 'being together', whether in a hall of residence, a lecture theatre or in the uni bar. Students live together, learn together and learn to live together. Togetherness is a precious currency in which students are expert dealers. From day one, when most students will arrive at a uni hall, there is a sense of starting a journey together. Almost all the students I have spoken to in the last few years were still good friends with at least one person they met within their first few hours as a student. Already, at this early stage, community is being built. Halls are a great place to make friends and to get to know people at a really deep level. You will know the people who live around you while you are at uni better than most other people in your life. Living in a small space together for a whole year is an intense experience that will create a deep bond between you and your friends, which will hold significance long after the year has finished.

Of course, we were all created to live in this way, but our society conditions us to be suspicious of strangers, and to remain detached and private from people we don't know very well. Only our family and closest friends are admitted into our inner circle of trust, in which we share who we really are and make ourselves vulnerable to other people. This reminds me of the film *Meet the Parents,* in which Ben Stiller plays a guy who goes to visit his girlfriend's parents for the weekend. Robert De Niro plays the father of the family, who also happens to be an ex-CIA agent. De Niro's character is suspicious of his daughter's boyfriend and goes to great lengths to make sure he is suitable for his little girl. When he thinks he is happy with Stiller's character he gives him a long speech about being welcomed into the circle of trust and becoming part of the family. Just to make sure he knows everything he should, he hooks Stiller up to a lie detector and interrogates him. It's a very funny scene, not least because it's not that far away from the truth. We are often slow to open our homes and lives to those around us, or to trust them to be on the inside of things we would rather keep private. Most of us feel more comfortable when we can lock the door (actually or metaphorically) and keep people we don't know very well out of our lives. This just isn't how life pans out as a student, and for some being more open with people can take a little getting used to. Gregarious natural relaters will do well at uni because people will like them and they will make friends quickly. If you are good at getting to know people, make sure you look out for those who aren't, as there are always one or two who get left out of the crowd in the first few days.

Freedom

My parents have a dog called Sweep. She is a beautiful black Labrador, and it's always great when I go home to be able to see her and take her for a walk. I have to walk for about five minutes before I get to some open country and can let the dog off the lead. For those five minutes Sweep will pull ahead, straining to be able to get to the fields and have a run. When I finally reach the edge of the field and bend down to remove her lead, she will duck through the loop before I've had a chance to loosen it properly and be off chasing around the field looking for trouble. She loves to be free.

The energy and vitality that Sweep has for her daily walk is pretty much the same as a typical student has for life when they first get to university. You will never have more freedom than this. As a teenager it can be frustrating having to obey your parents, go to school, do your homework and tidy your room. Even the independence you have experienced as a 17- and 18-year-old will probably not compare to the complete autonomy you experience when you first move to university. For three whole years no one will tell you what to do, unless you get into a relationship, of course!

The attitude of most students reflects the liberty they are allowed by life at university. There is a sense that you can do whatever you want, whenever you want, and with whomever you want. 'If it makes you happy, do it.' This is classic hedonism and studentdom is by and large a hedonistic culture. Many of the stereotypes associated with students, such as drink, drugs and sex, find this culture of freedom highly inducive, as students are able to experiment with their lifestyle in order to find out what makes them happy, all the time pushing the boundaries further and further back. Students are experts at living to excess, and freedom is the catalyst that allows them to do it.

If you are a Christian, you may feel that nothing could be further away from the lifestyle of Christianity than this part of student culture. However, I believe that freedom is a gift from God. Galatians 5:1 says, 'It is for freedom that Christ has set us free.' We are free because God has chosen to give us freedom. This can be seen right through Scripture, as God gives first Adam and Eve freedom in the Garden of Eden, and then his people freedom to choose to follow him. What then has Christ set us free from? Has he set us free from the world? Perhaps we are free from the need to please God? No. Jesus set us free from our slavery to sin and a future that leads to death. Students may say that they are free to drink as much as they can and sleep with whomever they like tonight. Christ says that you are free not to.

Transition

Studentdom is a departure lounge between one part of life and the next. Students enter as children, uncertain, inexperienced, but excited by what lies ahead. They leave as adults, more mature, confident and ready to take on the world. This is one of the most vital parts of student life, but one that receives little attention. Do not underestimate how much you will develop as a person while you are at uni. Not only will you learn more about your chosen subject and doubtless pick up skills that will serve you in a future career, you will also mature in character, losing some of your rough edges as you learn to live and work alongside thousands of others. Many students testify to the fact that they have grown more in their all-round personality while at uni than they have learned in their academic subject. University is preparation for the rest of life in every area you can think of. It is a journey, and like all journeys you need to know something of where the journey will lead you and what you can expect along the way.

Preparation is a key theme in many biblical characters' lives. Joseph's time serving Potiphar in Egypt, and then his years in prison (the story is told in Genesis 39–41), prepared him well to advise Pharaoh and interpret his dreams. Samuel's time as part of Eli's household taught him what it meant to listen to God and do what he was asking (1 Samuel 1–3). Even Jesus went through a lengthy period of preparation as a carpenter with his family before he set out for three years of public ministry leading to his crucifixion. Preparation, it seems, is always key if you are to go on to bigger things later in life.

Identity

Studentdom is a place to discover who you are. 'Who am I?', the question Moses asks of God in Exodus 3, is one of the most important questions a person can ask, and most people will ask it regularly throughout their lifetime. As a teenager, life is a journey of self-discovery, building on the foundational basics of self-identity a child learns during his or her early years. From about the age of eleven, children begin to establish their independence from their parents and siblings, all the time working out who they are in relation to the world around them. Patterns in schooling, friendship and interests reflect the shift from dependence to interdependence that is an integral part of becoming an adult. As a teenager nears adulthood they are normally firmly established as a unique, autonomous individual, but with limited experience and maturity as an adult. This is where studentdom comes in.

As a stage between life as a child and life as an adult, student life is well placed to develop and deepen a young person's understanding of who they are and what their place in the world may be. This (often unconscious) search for identity is key to the make-up of student life, explaining many of the social and behavioural signs of student culture mentioned earlier in this preface. Although identity is rarely spoken of among students at uni, by the end of your student life you will have a much firmer understanding of who you are, and a sense of confidence in how you relate to others and what contribution you are able to make to society.

If you are a Christian student going to university this is good news. Not only can you look forward to the journey of student life that will help you to understand yourself and your place in the world, you also have a helpful framework in which to place this information. You know that your ultimate identity as a human being and follower of Jesus is as a child of God. You know that you were created in the image of God as a unique and special person who has eternal significance and a faithful Father in heaven who cannot help but love you. Your identity is not based on what you can get, as is that of many people caught in a materialist push for self-significance, but on what you have been given: undeserved and unequalled love. Your identity is secure and this places you in a special position within studentdom. While all around you friends and course mates are on their own journey of self-discovery, you will be able to stand shoulder to shoulder with them and allow them to see what knowing God has meant in your life. Your security in who you are and how you are loved will speak volumes about the faith in Jesus that you profess when the opportunity arises. 'Always be prepared to give an answer to everyone who asks you to give the reason for the hope that you have' (1 Peter 3:15).

These four themes are common currency in student life in every university I have ever visited. Community, freedom, transition and identity are exploratory journeys that all students must and will navigate as they do their coursework, spend time with their friends, eat and drink, play sport, and think about their future. They are themes that are relevant in every chapter of this book, every lecture hall and lab, and every student corridor. For me they are what student life is all about, and they are all themes that a Christian student can engage with and bring some truth to.

The story of Daniel has a lot to teach the student fraternity. Daniel is a major biblical hero, but did you know that he went to uni? It's all in chapter 1 of his book in the Bible. Daniel lives with his mates in Jerusalem. A foreign king, with a very funny name, besieges the city to defeat the Israelites. In order to consolidate his victory, the king takes the next generation of leaders back to Babylon to train them to be his servants. Daniel and his three friends get taken as part of the deal.

It's a complete culture shock to them as they are forced to live in this foreign society. Everything changes for them, not unlike when students head off to uni. There are a number of issues on which Daniel has to make choices. He agrees to be trained in the language and literature of the Babylonians, and he allows his name to be changed to sound like one of the Babylonian gods. But then he draws the line. He refuses to eat and drink the food and wine the king has provided for him.

It's not that there was anything wrong with these things or that the things he allowed were entirely godly.

What we can learn from Daniel is that he made choices to honour God in the context of his character and identity, as the person God had made him and wanted him to be. Those choices are not the same for you and me, but the motive behind them should be the same: to put God first.

At university many students choose one of two approaches, neither of which is ideal. You can choose to look at student culture and see all that is ungodly about it, making sure you never get tainted by all the things Christians are supposed to steer clear of. It's low risk, but it's not going to save the world. Or you could choose to dive right in and be as much like those around you as possible, making sure your life is always relevant. The trouble is that soon you will get lost in the crowd and any ounce of credibility you once had as a Christian will fade away as your mates realise you are no different from them.

I believe there is a third option. You must be like Daniel, plotting a tough course between embracing student culture and making a stand when the line is breached. You will make mistakes, and that's OK. You will get criticised, and sometimes that can hurt. But at least you'll be real and start to make a difference. That's when something really exciting might happen!

1
application and
making decisions

Neo wasn't exactly sure what was happening. He had never been here before and everything was strange and unfamiliar. One moment he had known who he was and what he was doing, and the next everything was changing. And here he was faced with a choice – possibly the biggest he had ever had to make. It could change his life. It could take him to a place he'd never been before. Everything around him would change; he would enter a whole new world. It could even change *him*. So what would he do? How should he choose? How could he know how things would turn out? He had a decision to make. The red pill or the blue?

Life is full of decisions. Whether it's where we live, who we marry, whether to enter the matrix, or which uni to go to, somehow or other we have to choose. Studentdom is a place full of choices; just getting into the place forces each student into a maze of decisions. So how should you choose where to spend your student days? How can you decide which uni you should go to?

Studentdom is changing

Studentdom is no longer solely the choice of the elite. Its experiences and benefits are not limited to the chosen few any more. The government aims to make sure that by 2010 50 per cent of all school leavers enter higher education. The demographics of the student population of the UK have changed, as vast new sections of society have been given the opportunity to study beyond school. The twentieth century saw the greatest transformation of the higher education system since Oxford and Cambridge first opened their doors some 600 years ago. The advent of new universities throughout the century, such as Manchester and Sheffield, and the expansion of the system to include polytechnics and vocational colleges during the 1990s, created new opportunities for those previously beyond the reach of higher education. In 1993 the UCCA (Universities Central Council on Admissions) system covered just 95 institutions. The University and Colleges Admissions Service (UCAS) currently handles applications for 261 universities and colleges across the UK. New places have been created and entrance requirements for some courses lowered to attract more and more young people to university.

In the academic year 2000/01 just under 1.2 million

people were in full-time higher education at a university or college in the UK. A further 600,000 part-time students were studying on degree-level courses. The total number of students in the UK has been rising steadily each year; intake in September 2000 saw a 3 per cent increase. The student population is growing, and will continue to grow, as successive governments seek a broader education system. There are more international students in Britain than ever before. In some colleges those from other nations can make up more than 20 per cent of the total student population, and there are people from every nation in the world studying in our universities. The influence of our education system and the communities of our halls and bars spread further than we can imagine.

Studying at university and gaining a degree used to be a very special thing. Not everybody had the opportunity or was capable of working to this level. Now the system is much more inclusive and many more people are taking this option. There was a time when to have a degree meant you would have the pick of the jobs when leaving uni and be 'made for life'. Not so any more. Every other Fred has one, and interview rooms are full of 2:1s and MAs. Having a degree has almost become a necessity – the norm if you like. It might not be obvious at times, but there are other post-school options, and some people may be better off looking into other things.

Work

Many young people leave school aged 16, 17 or 18, get a job and begin their career. Some dislike the idea of uni, some don't make the grades they need to get on a course, and some just want to get out there, earn a crust and stop looking at books all day. I hear stories all the time of people who have left school and got a job, done well and been very successful in their career. Sometimes they succeed ahead of those in the same field who have a degree, but this is becoming rarer as higher education becomes the established benchmark. The advantages of moving into the workplace are that you will receive an income much earlier and have the opportunity to gain some experience and make some connections ahead of the graduate crowd. ▶▶ 16. career and vocation

Vocational training

It is possible to get some training towards an occupation without going to uni. This is true particularly of trades and practical skills. Occupations such as carpentry and childcare tend towards this type of training, as the more academic environment of university does not suit teaching these skills. The advantages of vocational training are that you tend to get into the job quicker, and the course is designed to train you to succeed in the field you have chosen.

Apprenticeships

An apprenticeship is similar to vocational training, but 'on the job'. Apprenticeships are available in most trades where it is essential to learn alongside someone with skills and experience in the field. Car mechanic and furniture-maker are good examples of trades that offer this type of training. The advantages of an apprenticeship are that the work is very practical and you are being paid as you train.

Travel

More and more school leavers want to see the world before they settle into a job. Some will work before they travel in order to pay for their extended holiday; others will leave as soon as possible and perhaps find casual work along the way. There are companies that specialise in this kind of adventure and will help you put it all together. It is worth thinking about what your options are for when you return and perhaps lining up a place at uni in advance. ▶▶ 13. holidays and travel

Higher education

One of the main reasons for going to uni is to get a qualification. It is becoming increasingly difficult to get into some jobs without a degree, and there are a few where the right letters after your name are essential. Having said all that there are a million other reasons for packing your bags and moving to a strange city for three years. Studentdom is a place of development, and not just in terms of how much you learn. It's a place to discover more about yourself, grow up and find out what life is all about. It's a place to make some great friends, try some new experiences and stretch your thinking. Above all, it's a place to become someone. That someone is you.

My advice to anyone considering going to university is this: have a think about all the options available to you and honestly weigh up which one you are most suited to. Too many people go the uni route just because it's the done thing. With something this big you have to think it through. It's important to bear in mind what you'd like to be doing in ten years' time, as well as where you'd like to be next week. If after thinking about it and talking it over with a few people who know you well you are confident uni is for you, then go for it. You can always change your mind later on!

The application process

Once you've decided you'd like to go to uni, you need to start the application process. This can take quite a while so you need to start thinking about it well in advance. If you are at school or sixth-form college the staff will give you plenty of advice and tell you when things need to be done. The whole process, no matter what university you apply to, is administered by a single agency called the University and Colleges Admissions Service (UCAS). While UCAS makes applying to university fairly straightforward, there are some complications to watch out for. If you decide to apply to Oxford or Cambridge, you will need to make sure your form has reached UCAS by 15 October to start the course the following autumn. You may not apply to both Oxford and Cambridge, but must choose between them, although you can add up to five other choices on your form. To study medicine, veterinary science or dentistry you also need to get the form in by 15 October, and you only get four choices on the form instead of the usual six. For most other universities and courses you have a little longer; the form must reach UCAS by 15 January, and you get all six choices. If you want to study art and design there are two routes of application you can take. Route A is exactly the same as for most other courses, i.e. you get six choices and the form needs to be in by 15 January. Route B restricts you to three choices (in preference order) and you need to apply between 1 January and 24 March. Each uni that offers an art and design course decides which route they want applicants to go through, and to make it even more confusing some let you apply through either route! Apart from Route B of art and design you don't need to specify any preference to your choices; you simply fill in the form in the order that your choices appear in the UCAS *Big Guide*, which is a directory/handbook for the whole system.

If you want to defer your entry by a year to take the

opportunity to travel, get some work experience or earn some money to pay for uni, you should still apply as if you were intending to start immediately, and tick the box to defer. Waiting until the next year to apply can cause problems later on, as you could be overseas when you need to communicate with UCAS, or you might have a change of heart during the summer and decide you want to go straight to uni after all. It is much better to have a place lined up and your grades in the bag. Then you can forget about it until the following summer. You can always change your mind, even after a place has been agreed, and most universities look favourably on gap years.

Choosing a course

Most schools and colleges provide a careers service to help you with your choices. They will have a number of copies of the UCAS *Big Guide*, which lists all the available course choices for the coming year. This changes every year, so make sure you are looking at the right one! Alternatively you could look at their website www.ucas.co.uk, which has a course search facility. You will normally start looking at courses and boiling down your choices a good six months before you finally send in the form. It is best to start with choosing your course first as they vary hugely from university to university. You can think about which uni to go to a little further down the line. So how do you make your choice?

1. What would you like to do as a job when you finish university? Knowing where you want to end up can be very helpful when deciding how you are going to get there. For some people this can make the course choice very simple because they need to study on a particular course to be able to work in a particular profession. It's no good studying geography if you want to be a doctor! For other people, there may be no obvious link between a course and a career, but there are some subjects that will help pave the way. For example, if you would like to go into the business sector when you finish uni, it might be a good idea to look into courses that teach skills used in business, such as finance, management or marketing.

2. Think about what you have enjoyed studying at school, what you are particularly good at and what you would like to do more of. If there is a subject you have really developed a strong interest in, you might like to continue to study this subject in greater depth at university. One of the advantages of higher education is that you will get the chance to specialise in a particular field, allowing you to go far further in your chosen subject than is possible at school. Some people never come to the end of their studies in a given subject and continue their learning and research throughout their whole lives!

3. Are there any natural skills and talents you would like to develop given the opportunity? School does not always allow these things to flourish, but university

can give you the chance to study something that is not on the National Curriculum. One example would be communication. Some people are very natural communicators, either in speaking or in the written word. Such a person could look into courses at uni that reflect this natural gift. Media, marketing, and teaching courses could all allow this talent to develop.

4. Who do you admire? Who would you like to emulate when you enter the workplace? A politician, entrepreneur, journalist, film-maker? University offers the chance to study almost anything you can think of. Why not pursue your dream and see where it takes you? You may just find that studying something a little more unusual could be very satisfying and lead you into the perfect career when you graduate!

All of these are good reasons to choose a particular course. It is worth taking some time to consider these things and any other factors you can think of, as your choices are likely to be important to your future.

Once you have some idea what kind of courses you are interested in, try and whittle them down to a short list of just a few different types of course. Check out what requirements you will need to get onto these courses and make sure you are likely to have what is being asked for. If you want to study medicine and have not been doing biology and chemistry at A-level, you are going to struggle to find a course that will sign you up. You will also need to start thinking about what exam grades you are likely to end up with, as these will have a dramatic effect on your chances too. Universities now tend to select students on the basis of their AS-level exams, which are taken after the first year of sixth form. These are the grades you will put down on the UCAS form, and they will show the universities you apply to how well you are likely to do in your A-levels a year later. With this in mind, it is essential to do your best for the AS exams, as well as the A-level exams, in order to secure the place you deserve at university.

Once you have checked these things out and have a short list, it's time to make some more decisions. Which of the options you have left really falls out of the pack? You are perfectly entitled to apply for completely different courses when you fill in the UCAS form, but it is probably best to plump for a particular type of course at this stage. Having a range of options on your form will show that you haven't made up your mind yet and are not committed to the course you are applying to. If you get offered places on different courses, you are going to have to decide which one you want to go on in the end anyway.

Which university should I go to?

Having decided which type of course you really want to study, you can begin to look into which universities offer that course. In looking at the course options, you have probably already built up some ideas of what is available where, and of the differences between each university. This is an important point to remember: an English literature course at one uni will be quite different from a course of the same title at another. Come up with a list of possible unis – you might select 10 or 15, depending on what course you want to study – and get hold of a copy of their prospectus: a concise guide to the uni and syllabuses for all the courses they offer. The careers centre at your school, college or library will have one for each uni, but you will not be able to take these away, so you may want to telephone each uni direct, or find their website, and get them to send you your own copy. Prospectuses are free and it is essential to have a good look at each one for your possible choices before making up your mind.

One word of warning here: remember that the prospectus is a piece of publicity trying to sell something. The product is the uni and the course; the customer is you. Try and read between the lines a little and think about what they don't tell you, as well as what they have spent thousands of pounds to draw your attention to.

The prospectuses should help you get your list down nearer to the final number of choices you are allowed to submit. Some universities host a uni fair, to which other unis are invited to come and talk to students. You can get all the prospectuses you want at one of these. It is worth asking around a little at this stage to find out what others think about your choices. You may know people who have been to the universities you are considering. You can visit universities when they have an Open Day, and also have a good look around their website to get an idea of what the place is like.

Open Days are a good opportunity to talk to some of the students there and get a feel for the atmosphere, facilities and accommodation. Don't try to go to too many of these, as they take a whole day and can be rather draining. Again remember that the staff and students you meet are trying to give you the very best impression of their uni, and are paid to do so. Yes, that's right – the students who participate in Open Days are usually paid for their time. You will probably leave each university with a mixture of good and bad impressions.

Universities hold Open Days throughout each academic year. You will need to plan to visit unis during the middle of your sixth form in order to get the benefit of Open Days before you submit your UCAS form. It is worth pointing out that you can also pop in on any other day of the year too, as uni campuses are open to the public, but you will not benefit from a guided tour and may be prevented from entering some buildings.

When choosing which uni you want to study at, you should bear in mind a number of factors that may affect your decision:

1. Do they offer the course you want to study? It may sound obvious, but there is no point setting your

heart on a particular location if they cannot teach you what you want to learn. It is fairly common to choose a uni first and see what courses they offer, but I would advise against this as the course is the main difference between universities. Everything else is largely replicated at every uni.

2. Is the university a good choice for the course you want to study? Unis are a little like restaurants. Although they all look and feel quite similar, they serve very different dishes. Unis tend to specialise in certain types of courses and will have established a reputation for delivering the goods in that field. Most unis will have a good range of courses and cover all the main subjects, but some are better than others for certain things. You might think that older, more famous universities would be the best in every field, but this is no longer true. Some smaller, newer and less prestigious establishments are often world leaders in their specialist fields.

3. Where is the university located? Depending on where you live, and what kind of town or city appeals to you, you may have a preference in location. Some people want to live at home or be near to their home, so they can pop back frequently and get Mum to do a couple of loads in the Hotpoint! Others prefer to move further away and be a little more independent. You may like the vibe of a particular city and want to live there for a few years. As long as you don't make this the only criterion to influence your

decision, it can be a useful thing to think about.

4. Is the university based on a campus or in a city? There are two main types of uni. There are those based on a single campus site (sometimes two or three campuses are used), usually a little way out of the city centre (e.g. Essex), and those that have departments and buildings spread out over an area of a city, usually nearer the centre and very much part of the city itself (e.g. Manchester).

5. Do you know anyone else at the university? Knowing someone else at the uni of your choice can be really helpful. They can give you some insight into what it is like to live and study as part of this community, and can show you the ropes when you first turn up. You may prefer, however, to go it alone and experience everything for yourself, first hand.

6. What facilities does the university have? As I have already said, most unis offer very similar facilities, and choosing between them on this basis can be misleading. They will all have a Student Union, a shop, sports facilities, bars and cafés, university halls and a host of other services provided to help and entertain your student life. It is well worth checking out the halls and other accommodation options and finding out how much they cost, as these things can make a difference to your choice.

Having taken some time to weigh up the pros and cons of different courses and universities, you can fill in and send off your UCAS form. It will take several months for all the universities to get back to you, and there are a number of responses they could make. They could ask you to come and visit them for an interview, they could offer you a place on the condition that you get certain grades in your exams (or that your grades add up to a specified number of points), or they could decline your application. Most people get some of their choices rejected, so don't worry if that happens to you. I had five rejections before I was finally offered a place!

If you are called to an interview, you will be given a date and a time to visit the uni and meet with one of the tutors who works for that university. For some courses, such as teaching, interviews are obligatory. Although this can be daunting, it is not unusual and is not something to get worked up about. You should dress reasonably smartly and think about what you want to say about yourself and your reasons for wanting to study at that particular university. They will probably not require you to do any other preparation (they will tell you very clearly if they do) and will simply expect you to be on time, polite and, most important of all, yourself. You should hear back from the uni within a few weeks of the interview.

If you are offered a place, you need do nothing immediately. Wait until you have a response from all the universities you have applied to. When you know which unis have offered you a place, you will need to decide on a first choice and a reserve choice. For your first choice you should choose the place you most want to take, and the one where you are likely to be able to meet the requirements of the offer. You need to believe in your best, but be realistic. Some unis only offer accommodation in halls to students who choose that uni as their first choice, so there could be a sting in the tail if you don't do as well in your exams as you expected. Your reserve choice is a back up in case you do not get the grades you need for your first choice. You should choose a place that requires lower grades, but one you are still happy to take if needs be.

If you do not receive any offers, don't panic! You may be able to reapply, and will certainly be able to get a place through the clearing process during the summer. This is when all the untaken places and all the students still to find a place are matched up. Very few people who really want to go to uni fail to make it, so whatever happens along the way, there is always another door to push! If once you have your exam results you are a few points short of what you have been offered, it is worth phoning the university to see if they will still take you, because often they will. Once you have arrived at uni you can still decide to change course or university if you are not happy.

Making decisions is never easy and it is wise to take your time, listen to good advice from others, and pray over your choices. Once you have made your decision, be confident that you have done all you can, and trust that the outcome will be a good one! Then you can relax and concentrate on passing your exams. The application process is deliberately started early to give everyone plenty of time to do what needs to be done and to leave the period immediately before exams clear for you to revise and do as well as you possibly can.

2

leaving home

There was a car advert on TV a while ago that showed a family getting ready to go on a journey. Once they had everything ready they jumped in the shiny car and hit the road. As the camera panned back you saw their little boy left behind at the house – they had forgotten to take him with them. After a few minutes Mum and Dad realised their mistake and returned to the house to pick up the little guy, embarrassed that in their excitement about what lay ahead they had forgotten to take care of the most important thing!

Leaving home is a big deal and it can be easy to get carried away in the excitement of the journey without making sure you have thought about everything properly before you go. Once you walk out of that door, things will never be the same again. It is a watershed, a landmark on the journey of life. For some people it happens when they get married. One day they are young, free, single and living at home; the next they are older, committed and hitched. Others leave home when a job calls them further afield, or they simply get fed up with home cooking and fresh laundry. However, for an increasing number of young people, the reason they are wrenched from the family abode is nothing more than education; they are leaving home to go to university. It's true they may return, at least during the holidays and possibly when they graduate, but home will not be the same. The day you leave home heading for studentdom is a momentous day.

You may not have thought leaving home was such a big issue. Most people concentrate their thoughts on what is to come at university and not on what they are leaving behind. This is very natural, and it is important to think ahead to your time at uni and anticipate some of the experiences you will have there. We'll come to that, but for now there are a few things closer to home we need to look at.

Moving on

Leaving home is not simply about packing up your treasured belongings, saying your goodbyes and heading for the door. It is an important moment in the life of any young adult, a signpost along the path between childhood and adulthood. When you go to university, it can feel as though you are in a distinct world between these two states of being. It's a bit like the Dartford Tunnel: once you enter the tunnel you are neither north nor south of the River Thames, but somehow in the middle.

If studentdom marks the end of childhood, it's obvious that there is more to it than simply a change of location. The whole point of childhood is that it is a journey to becoming an adult, picking up all you need to succeed when you get there along the way. You can't be a child for ever, and most of us don't want to be. Naturally as children we always want to be older than we are and take more responsibility for ourselves than we have had before. It's this desire that propels us through our teenage years. Once we have left childhood behind us, sometimes we wish we could return and live again in the comfort and stability that that environment provides. I can't count the number of times I have come across a difficult issue as a young adult and wished things could be as simple as I remember them being when I was 14.

Going deeper

Leaving home heralds a new season. We are no longer confined to a limited number of relationships and experiences. The doors of adult life are thrown open and we have instant access to a whole load of new stuff designed to keep us amused. I see this as moving into deeper water:

When [Jesus] had finished speaking, he said to Simon, 'Put out into deep water, and let down the nets for a catch.'

Simon answered, 'Master, we've worked hard all night and haven't caught anything. But because you say so, I will let down the nets.'

When they had done so, they caught such a large number of fish that their nets began to break. So they signalled to their partners in the other boat to come and help them, and they came and filled both boats so full that they began to sink. (Luke 5:4–7)

Jesus is right at the beginning of the three years he spent with his disciples, and this is one of the first times that he and Simon Peter have met. Simon is naturally suspicious when Jesus tries to give him some fishing tips. You see, Jesus had grown up helping his dad in the carpentry workshop. He wasn't a fisherman, and I don't think his simple advice impressed Simon very much. Simon had been up all night, trying all his best tricks to get the fish to bite, and then this guy turns up and makes a suggestion. Can you imagine what Simon thought? 'Oh OK, because *you* say so, we'll try over there.' You can almost hear him saying under his breath, 'What does he know about fishing?' But sure enough, when Simon does as Jesus says and heads for the deeper water, he gets his reward: a massive catch of fish.

The fact is, Jesus knows when we should put out into deeper water. Paddling around in childhood is good for a while, but when we want to land a bigger catch we have to head out into the deeper parts of life. It's more dangerous, harder to work out where the fish are, and we may need a bit of advice along the way, but the result is worth it. That's exactly what leaving home is all about: leaving the calm shallow waters and heading into deeper seas. As the designer and sustainer of human life, Jesus knows which bit of water we should head into and what we will find when we get there. Just as Simon Peter and his mates did after their fishing trip, it's worth thinking about whether you want Jesus with you as you navigate through your student life.

All that you can't leave behind

Leaving home is not all about what you are heading for though. It can be about what you are leaving behind. Some people have an unhappy childhood and when they look back there are things they would rather leave behind for good. It can be a very painful part of life, and in this way leaving home can also be a big issue. It can be an opportunity to move away from a difficult situation or to make a fresh start. New opportunities and challenges lie ahead, but for some people the biggest challenges they will face are behind them.

These things don't just go away when you physically leave the building you have grown up in. Your parents are still your parents, no matter how many miles separate you, and it probably won't help to run away from a difficult situation at home. If at all possible it is better to deal with things so that you feel free to move on and enjoy the next part of your life. If you have found home life difficult, and you are able to, take some time to talk things over with your family and friends, and try to find a way to bring some resolution to the situation. Forgiveness and communication are very powerful tools, and their effect over time should not be underestimated.

Leaving home is also an independence day. This can be quite a shock to the system. Suddenly you have complete responsibility for yourself, and all decisions are yours to make. No one is going to tell you what time to come home, when to do your work or what to watch on TV. Equally you are going to have to fend for yourself in the kitchen and the laundry, and ensure you have enough cash to make it to the end of the month. It's no secret that this new-found liberty can lead even the most conscientious of teenagers to make a mistake or two in the first few weeks at uni. Funnily enough, the advice and discipline your parents have offered over the years has more than likely been for your benefit and helped to make you the all-round superstar you are now, so it's worth thinking it through if you are planning to go wild. I'm not saying there is anything wrong with letting your hair down a bit once you are off the reins, but don't do something stupid just because you can!

Expect things to change

It's important to think about what will change when you

leave home. In many ways this can depend on the individual, but there are some common themes that come up for many young people as they pack their belongings for the first time.

Expect your relationships to change. Living at home with your mum, dad, brothers and sisters is one thing. You've done it for the last 18 years and it feels normal. They are always there and so are you. Sometimes you get on like a house on fire and sometimes you don't. It's natural – we call it family. Then one day you leave for uni and when you come back it can feel a bit weird. The people are the same and pretty much everything is in the same place, but somehow it feels different – almost like being a visitor in your own home. Now you have loads to talk about because you are not living in each other's pockets all the time. The mundane becomes interesting because it's not happening under your nose like it used to. You have to understand that you will change over the time you are away, so it's no wonder your relationships at home will change too. It's almost as though your mum and dad become your friends instead of your parents. You might even start to like your siblings again too!

Parents can find it tough when their children go to uni, and you should not expect all the support in the family to flow in one direction at this time. Regular communication with home is essential for you and your folks as you all get used to the change in circumstances. Your parents will probably feel the need to talk to you more than you do with them, so be considerate and make sure they know you still think about them. It's not easy for them to know what's going on with you at uni, so take time to tell them about your student life and be sure to let them know when anything bothers you. They may have expectations for your lifestyle which you think are unrealistic, but if you talk about these things before and during your time at uni you will find a lot of common ground. Pray for your parents as they adjust to home without you. It can be hard for them to let you leave the nest, and strange to have extra time to spend with each other.

A new way of seeing things

Expect your worldview to change. At home you will have picked up a perspective on life; one angle on the great adventure. There are plenty of other ways of looking at things out there, and when you leave home, especially if you're going to uni, you will bump into a few new opinions. It's not that one thing is wrong and another is right – they're just different. It's part of the rich tapestry of life. When you go to uni you will come across all kinds of weird and wonderful outlooks on life, some of which you will agree with and some you will not. In a way that is what university is all about: stretching and maturing the way you think, and helping you to think for yourself. I've known people in their first few weeks at uni who can talk on every subject as though they're an expert, but when you ask them why they think the way they do, they admit they've picked it up from their parents. There is nothing wrong with respecting what your parents say about life, but it's not a bad idea to find out for yourself and decide what you think. Uni is a great opportunity to do that. You have to remember though, when you go home, that you have a load of new ideas in your head. Chances are your folk haven't changed much and they may find you a bit of a handful if you overdo telling them everything you've picked up while you have been away.

▶▶ 6. study and coursework

Confident?

This leads us nicely to the area of confidence. Expect your belief in yourself to rise when you get some exposure to other worldviews. Finding out more about what you think, and therefore more about who you really are, is likely to make you feel a lot more sure of yourself. Experience breeds confidence. A lot of young people have an air of self-assurance about them that borders on qualifying them for a diploma in arrogance. The thing is that when you get a chance to try it out for real, you find out what is and what isn't. This means that although you will be humbled in some areas, in others you will emerge with real confidence. Confidence that is based on experience is worth a thousand times more than that which remains a theory.

Getting away from home for a while forces you into the type of environment where some of your life skills are going to get a pretty serious road test. There's nothing like it, and no short cut, but it's the stuff adult life is made of. Expect those who know you well to be surprised, when you come home in the holidays, by just how much more assured you seem to be. By the time you leave uni you will be a Jedi master in the art of experience-based life skills, ready to tackle whatever comes next.

You will always be you

There is one thing that won't change when you leave home. In fact it will never change, no matter what you do. You will always be you. Unique, special and loved by God – one of a kind. You were created to be you. You are meant to be you. Your first job every day, the task at the very top of your 'to do' list, is to be you. You will never really change; you will just become more of who you really are. As a Christian this means that you have discovered your identity as a child of God and feel secure in the confidence that brings. This can be a comfort when you leave home because a lot of the things around you will be changing. You will change where you live and what you do every day. Your friends will change and the relationships you've had before going to uni will change too. Your opinions and worldview will be challenged, and your ideas will develop. Despite all of this turbulence, when all the furniture of life is being rearranged around you, in the middle of it all stands you. That's the way God made you and he loves you for it.

O LORD, you have searched me and you know me. You know when I sit and when I rise; you perceive my thoughts from afar. You discern my going out and my lying down; you are familiar with all my ways. Before a word is on my tongue you know it completely, O LORD. You hem me in – behind and before; you have laid your hand upon me. Such knowledge is too wonderful for me, too lofty for me to attain. Where can I go from your Spirit? Where can I flee from your presence? If I go up to the heavens, you are there; if I make my bed in the depths, you are there. If I rise on the wings of the dawn, if I settle on the far side of the sea, even there your hand will guide me, your right hand will hold me fast. If I say, 'Surely the darkness will hide me and the light become night around me,' even the darkness will not be dark to you; the night will shine like the day, for darkness is as light to you. For you created my inmost being; you knit me together in my mother's womb. I praise you because I am fearfully and wonderfully made; your works are wonderful, I know that full well. My frame was not hidden from you when I was made in the secret place. When I was woven together in the depths of the earth, your eyes saw my unformed body. All the days ordained for me were written in your book before one of them came to be. (Psalm 139:1–16)

3

starting uni and
freshers week

During the night after his first day, Marcus woke up every half-hour or so. He could tell from the luminous hands of his dinosaur clock: 10.41, 11.19, 11.55, 12.35, 12.55, 1.31 . . . He couldn't believe he was going to have to go back there the next morning, and the morning after that, and the morning after that, and . . . well, then it would be the weekend, but more or less every morning for the rest of his life, just about. Every time he woke up his first thought was that there must be some kind of way past, or round, or even through, this horrible feeling; whenever he had been upset about anything before, there had usually turned out to be some kind of answer – one that mostly involved telling his mum what was bothering him. But there wasn't anything she could do this time. She wasn't going to move him to another school, and even if she did it wouldn't make a whole lot of difference. He'd still be who he was, and that, it seemed to him, was the basic problem.

He just wasn't right for schools. Not secondary schools, anyway. That was it. And how could you explain that to anyone? It was OK not to be right for some things (he already knew he wasn't right for parties, because he was too shy, or for baggy trousers, because his legs were too short), but not being right for school was a big problem. Everyone went to school. There was no way around it. Some kids, he knew, got taught by their parents at home, but his mum couldn't do that because she went out to work. Unless he paid her to teach him – but she'd told him not long ago that she got three hundred and fifty pounds a week from her job. Three hundred and fifty pounds a week! Where was he going to get that kind of money from? Not a paper round, he knew that much. The only other kind of person he could think of who didn't go to school was the Macaulay Culkin kind. They'd had something about him on Saturday morning TV once, and they said he got taught in a caravan sort of thing by a private tutor. That would be OK, he supposed. Better than OK, because Macaulay Culkin probably got three hundred and fifty pounds a week, maybe even more, which meant that if he were Macaulay Culkin he could pay his mum to teach him. But if being Macaulay Culkin meant being good at drama, then forget it: he was crap at drama, because he hated standing up in front of people. Which was why he hated school. Which was why he wanted to be Macaulay Culkin. Which was why he was never going to be Macaulay Culkin in a thousand years, let alone in the next few days. He was going to have to go to school tomorrow.

(Taken from *About a Boy* by Nick Hornby. Published by Indigo, an imprint of Orion, 1999.)

Starting something new can be a bit daunting, especially while you are getting to know other people in the first few days. It can be a bit manic, with loads to do in the week or so before you go. You might worry about what it's going to be like, whether you'll make friends, or how you are going to pay for it. Maybe you'll even think once or twice before you go that you don't want to go at all! This is all very normal. The fact of the matter is: going to uni is fun. It is one of those once in a lifetime, never forgotten, make sure you tell your grandchildren type of experiences. You only do it once, and it comes with its own gift-wrapped set of unique challenges and worries. Leaving home, starting a new course, making new friends, living in a new place, learning to look after yourself . . . the list goes on. You will never do anything like it again, so enjoy it while you can!

Don't worry

Despite the fact that beginning student life is fun, anxiety is perfectly normal. Everyone worries a little bit. For some people, though, worry can make them very unhappy. It can feel as if an enormous weight is suspended above your head by a tiny thread, just waiting to squash you to the size of a pea. Going to uni is bound to bring this out in most people because a lot of uncertainty lies ahead. It is best to succumb to the reality that you cannot control everything, because the chances are everything will be OK, and however much you worry it's going to happen anyway. Jesus once said something about this:

> Therefore I tell you, do not worry about your life, what you will eat or drink; or about your body, what you will wear. Is not life more important than food, and the body more important than clothes? Look at the birds of the air; they do not sow or reap or store away in barns, and yet your heavenly Father feeds them. Are you not much more valuable than they? Who of you by worrying can add a single hour to his life? (Matthew 6:25–27)

Worry can disable us from functioning properly and enjoying the life we are living at the moment, as we become obsessed about the uncertainty of the future. Anxiety has its place as an inbuilt system in all of us to cause us to think carefully about the decisions we have to make, and to alarm us when something is wrong. This can be an overactive sense though, which paralyses us for fear of what may or may not happen, often in circumstances beyond our control. Jesus reminds us that we are not ultimately in control of anything; it is only God who has all things under his control.

This can be quite a releasing thought. If we are not in control, we do not have to take full responsibility for what is to come, and maybe we won't worry about it as much. It isn't down to us to make sure every minute detail turns out right. Perhaps we can learn to trust that God is on the case.

A friend of mine, who is a psychologist, says that he believes we are only in control of about 15 per cent of what comes at us during the course of an average day. The rest is determined by factors beyond our control. No matter which way you look at it, we certainly cannot control everything!

Jesus also reminds us of a very important point about worry: it doesn't really get us very far. Research has shown us again and again that worry and stress cause health problems. When was the last time you heard of worry being recommended as a key to longer life?

Be prepared

Going to uni can take a bit of preparation, so it's worth thinking about a few things before you go. Assuming you've applied and got a place sorted, you'll need to make sure there is somewhere for you to live when you get there. When your chosen uni confirms your place, they should send you some instructions on what you need to do to arrange your accommodation. Most unis have halls where the majority of first-years are able to live, although in the London universities it is becoming more difficult to secure a place in halls, as the student population is growing so rapidly. You will probably be able to indicate a preference as to what type of digs you'd like, but by no means does this guarantee where you'll end up. If there are not enough places in halls, you will be given contact information for housing agencies or some kind of student housing service that will help you find a house to share with some other students. Regardless of the type of accommodation available, this should be a well-trodden path by scores of students over the years, so you should have no problem. If you do find it difficult to get a place sorted, try and speak to the Student Union direct and they will be able to advise you on what to do. ▶▶ **4. halls and houses**

If your hall is self-catered, or you are going to be living in a house, you need to think about food too. It's not a bad idea to buy a few weeks' supplies before you leave home, so that you don't have to think about it for a while when you first get to uni. An additional bonus with doing it this way is that friendly relatives may choose to pay at the checkout, saving you a few quid for other 'essentials'. Even if you are getting all your meals in with the hall fees, you will want to stock up on a few extras. Tea, squash, snacks, biscuits, fruit, a few tins to put in the cupboard, and personal hygiene products will all come in handy in the weeks to come. You never know when you might want something to eat and the canteen isn't open. Most student accommodation comes with a kitchen with all the usual fittings, so you will be able to cook something whenever you feel peckish.

Your new home

When you arrive at uni you will go straight to your accommodation and settle in there. In halls almost everyone else will be new too, so you are all in the same boat. Find your room and unload your belongings as quickly as you can. If you are sharing a room, you will probably meet your room-mate soon after arriving. Spend a few minutes introducing yourself and your parents before you get into the unpacking. Once your parents have helped you get everything out of the car, and have had their first nose around of where you'll be living, it is usually a good idea to encourage them to leave you to it. You'll find it a lot easier to chat with the other students and make friends once they have left for home. This can be a tricky little moment, saying good-bye for the first time. You might want to walk them back to their car and say a quick goodbye there. That way you can make sure they have definitely gone!

The first day and night at uni will pass very quickly. You would be superhuman if you were not nervous. It will take a few hours to make friends with the people who live around you, but normally by the time the first evening comes you will have met most of them and got those first introductions under your belt. As you unpack your belongings in your room, it is a very good idea to keep your door open so that you meet the passers-by and get a feel for who is around. This is not just for your benefit. It sends out a message saying loud and clear, 'My door is open and I want to be friends with you.' It can make a lot of difference.

In halls there will usually be a meal, or at the very least a welcome meeting, put on soon after you arrive. Here the warden and staff of the hall will give you some basic information about where you are going to live. Once this has finished, it wouldn't be a university hall if the bar did not open. Almost everyone will head there to have a few drinks and meet their fellow hall-mates. This is a great opportunity to get to know people better, and is a must if you want to be a part of hall life from the start. As people relax, more of their natural character will come out and you will see more of who they really are. Some people will go totally over the top, get completely drunk and end up in the wrong bed for the night. That's how reputations are started. Of course it's entirely up to you, but I'd take it easy that first night and make sure I didn't do anything I'd regret for the rest of the year!

The first week of every university year, and your first week in studentdom, is known as Freshers Week, after the American word for a first-year. Lectures normally won't start until the following week, so there isn't a lot of work for you to do. This week is designed as a time for you to get to grips with uni life, settle into your accommodation, and find your way around the uni buildings.

You will be required to register for your course and meet some of the staff from the department you intend to study in. Every course is different, so we'll not go into any details about registration here. Simply follow the instructions your faculty gives you and you'll be fine. Apart from the academic side of Freshers Week, much of the action centres on the Student Union (SU), usually found at the heart of the uni. The SU exists to provide for the social needs of students while they are at university, and you will find it to be the hub of many student activities. ▶▶ 12. the student union and societies

Freshers Fair

During Freshers Week the SU will host a Freshers Fair for a few days to showcase all SU activities and societies. Here you will find a multitude of stalls designed to attract you to join a society or sports club. You'll see all kinds of weird and wonderful activities represented, giving you the opportunity to have a go at something new, usually either free or at a very reasonable price. Banks, shops, pubs and clubs are also represented here, so you'll be able to build up a good picture of what is available to you while you are at uni. One word of warning: all of the stall-holders at Freshers Fair are there to sell you something or sign you up for their club, so go easy on what you commit yourself to. You should be able to walk away from Freshers Fair with a bag full of freebies and the knowledge that anything you have signed up for is something you really want to do. This will not be the last opportunity to contact any of these organisations, so don't worry if you'd prefer to wait and see if you have the time or the need to talk to them later. Freshers Fair will probably be your first opportunity to meet people from various Christian groups represented on campus. You may not be sure what you want to get involved in, but it's definitely a good idea to go and say hello in the first week and find out what is going on so you can join in later on.

The other main focus of Freshers Week is the evenings. Every night there will be a different event, arranged either centrally on campus or in the uni halls, or both. Hall events tend to be very informal, organised by students and loads of fun. Typical examples would be silly games, Karaoke or a traffic light party. These evenings are fuelled by vast amounts of cheap alcohol, but in the most part offer great entertainment. The events the SU organises will be a bit more formal and more expensive, but just as much fun. They tend to be club events, parties and balls, often based on different themes, and will mostly be ticketed. It's worth checking out at least one or two of these, as they are usually very good, but pace yourself – it's only the first week! Local clubs and student societies may also arrange their own events, so there is more than enough to choose from, whatever your taste. Very few students will stay at home for these evenings, so even if you are not into the pub/club scene make a bit of an effort to spend time with your new friends, whatever they decide to do.

Freshers Week is one of the best parts of life at uni and I would encourage you to make the most of it. You have probably heard lots of stories of what this time can be like and what to steer clear of. It can be hard to know where to dive in and where to hang back. The important thing is that you are given the opportunity to make these decisions for yourself. Some of these stereotypes may be proved true, but in other cases there will not be a problem. My friend, Emma, describes her first week at uni like this:

'It was a really good experience; you meet so many people in a short space of time and go out with them. You get to know people so fast! There is a lot of alcohol, but there was less of an expectation to drink than I thought there would be, but everyone does. Everything is so cheap – the alcohol, clubs, taxis – and the focus is on enjoying yourself with your new friends. Although a lot of drugs do take place at uni, I don't remember any during Freshers Week. Everyone came with their own ideas of how to behave and there were some one-night stands, but that was the minority. I was surprised how much people's main focus was on making friends and having fun.'

Important things to bear in mind

To help you find your way through the maze of choices in your first days at uni, there are some things you should think about.

Who are you?

First, remember who you are. Uni can be an assault on your identity, constantly challenging you to compromise who you are in order for you to be like everyone else. If there is one thing worth learning in life, it is this: you must be yourself. No matter how much you try, or what changes you make, in the end you can only be you. Anything else is false and people will see through it. If you are a Christian you perhaps know more about your identity than those around you know about theirs. You know you are God's child, created in his image, to love him and be loved by him. You know that there is nothing you can do to make him love you any more or any less, and you know that you are different from everyone else around you. Not just because you are a Christian, but because God creates each of us to be unique.

Some people spend all their time trying to be something they are not. They try all day, every day to convince their friends they are X when they will always be Y. This reminds me of a story in the Old Testament. In 1 Samuel 8, the Hebrew people came to their leader, the priest Samuel, and asked him to choose a king to rule over them when he died. God had not intended for the people to have a king and saw their request as an insult because he wanted them to rely on him to lead and rule over them. He told Samuel they had rejected him as their king, and gave him a message to pass on to the people so that they might reconsider. However, the people looked around them at the other nations and saw that they all had kings, so they too wanted a king. In the end God gave in, saying to Samuel, 'Listen to them and give them a king.' The king Samuel appointed, a man named Saul, turned out to be a terrible leader, and all the bad things God had said would happen came true because they had not taken his advice.

In the same way God does not intend Christians to be the same as everyone else. He wants us to be different because of him. Sometimes it is easy for us to look around and want the things that others have. At uni this can be really hard, as many of our friends may get drunk, have a number of casual sexual relationships and generally behave in a way that we find difficult. It may be that sometimes we wish we could be like this too. The pressure to conform can be enormous, but remember this: your identity is secure and you can be different, love God and still hold the respect of your mates.

Making friends

Second, invest in friendship from day one. Getting to know people in the first few weeks at uni can be a challenge, but it is essential for your long-term happiness. Even with all that is going on, it is possible to feel quite lonely when you don't know people very well. Spending time talking, showing interest in your new friends' lives and backgrounds can make all the difference. Why not be the person who makes an effort to get to know people, goes out of their way to draw people in, and looks out for those who find it more difficult? At some point there is bound to be tension and people will fall out. Be ready to forgive easily and be a peacemaker when tempers fray, and you will go a long way. It takes longer to make a friend than an enemy, but I know which I'd rather have. ▶▶ 8. **friends and community**

Social religion

Third, make significant contact with another Christian student. It's easy to let the weeks go by at uni without getting involved in any Christian activities and quickly find yourself struggling without any Christian mates to support you. John Wesley said that Christianity was a social religion, which couldn't be lived alone, and he was dead right. Make sure you find out what is happening in the Christian groups on campus and go along to a few of the meetings arranged for your benefit. It is a great idea to arrange to meet one of the leaders or an older student for a coffee in the first few weeks so that you get to know someone early on. Having said all that, please don't just hang out with Christians and avoid everyone else. You will need a healthy mix of friends to be who Jesus wants you to be. ▶▶ 15. christianity on campus

Know your limits

Fourth, know your personal limits. Excess abounds at uni and your morals will be stretched. Some people get into difficulties because they haven't thought about what they want and don't want to do in certain situations. Alcohol and sex are the two major danger areas. Thinking about how much, if at all, you want to drink, and who you want to have a relationship with, before you are faced with these choices can help you avoid making a mistake later on. One friend of mine decided before he went to uni that he would not drink any alcohol during his first term. Someone else I know decided that she would not get into a relationship of any kind with a boy in her first term at uni so that she spent her time getting to know people in her hall. Both of them stuck to their decision. These kinds of decisions can be helpful, but whichever way you choose to approach these issues, some time spent thinking about how you will behave might save you some serious embarrassment further down the line.

Starting uni is a great experience and a time of many opportunities. If you are well prepared and confident in your identity, and you think before you act, you will have a ball. Then all the hard work begins!

4

halls and houses

If you have ever been on a camp, you already have a
pretty good idea of what life in halls is like. On
a recent trip to the United States I was the speaker on a
camp that took place in the mountains overlooking the
city of Denver. The campsite was an incredible place,
with forests, lakes, log cabins and a toboggan run that
we used well over the few days we were up there. During
our weekend together it was amazing to see how well
the group got to know each other and how deep our
friendships became. Those who had known each other
for a while seemed to step into a whole new level of
friendship, while those who were meeting for the first
time had the chance to form a strong bond in just a few
days. Living together creates an environment that helps
people to get to know each other in a way that they
cannot do when they meet for only a few hours each

week. It is this dynamic that makes life in uni halls very special.

Most students will spend at least one year of their time at university living in a hall of residence. Halls are large accommodation units, typically housing up to 1,000 students, which provide reasonably priced living space and the basic facilities needed to look after yourself as a student. The rooms are normally fairly small, with just enough room for a bed, desk and wardrobe, and are arranged in corridors, often with shared bathrooms and a kitchen. Most halls will have a larger space where students can congregate, either to eat meals, have hall meetings, or hold social events. There should also be a bar for the times when you want to relax and can't be bothered to venture very far, and a laundry to make sure you don't have to go home too often to get your washing done.

Once you have a place confirmed at a university, details about your accommodation should follow. You will get some opportunity to indicate a preference as to what type of room you would like, but mostly the choice of where you are to live for the next year will be made for you. You can expect to pay around £2,500 a year for catered accommodation, but fees vary quite a lot in different parts of the country and according to what standard of room you are given. The university prospectus should give some information about the halls of residence and an idea of current hall fees. Many students also choose to visit one of the university halls during an

Open Day, and this can often influence their preference to the extent that they end up living in the Hall they have visited.

Learning to live together

Living in halls is a fantastic experience, and many students will look back on these days as one of their favourite times. This is a place where lifelong friendships are often made. The vast majority of my friends who have been to university and graduated some time ago have at least one close friend from their time in halls. Life does not afford us many opportunities to live in such close proximity to people who aren't members of our family for such a long period of time. This is why they have such an impact on the lives of the students who inhabit them. Halls provide an environment in which students learn more about community, friendship, conflict, tolerance, patience and forgiveness than at any other point in their lives. During student life many young people are transformed from inexperienced children to confident young adults. This rapid change is due to the challenges and experiences studentdom puts in the path of each and every student, one of the most significant of which is life in halls.

One of the most fascinating aspects of life in a uni hall is the fact that you have virtually no choice as to who you live with when you are first allocated a place, especially when applying as a first-year. You can literally be placed with anyone. Not only will a typical hall community be made up of students from different social, educational and religious backgrounds, but more than likely there will also be a good number of international students added into the mix. It was quite a surprise to me when I first started living in halls how different people could be. I lived in a large house, annexed to a university hall, which had space for about 16 people. There were some single and some shared rooms, three shared bathrooms and a kitchen. We also had a resident sub-warden living in the largest room in the house, who you could be sure would have a word if we made too much noise. Among this group of 16 lads there was a tremendous variety of style, character and upbringing. By and large we got on pretty well, but at times it was a challenge. As we got to know each other, our opinions were expressed, our prejudices came out and we still had to share the same house every day.

Living in halls is a powerful experiment in community. Learning to live with the habits, preferences and weaknesses of other people is not easy. The majority of students, having lived as part of one community unit for at least 18 years, are fairly set in their ways and know what they are comfortable with. Of course, not everyone is the same, and students have not all had the same experiences, so when they come together and live in a corridor or house, it takes some getting used to. Those who are willing to be tolerant and patient, and try to see the positive side to others' personalities, will find it easier to fit into this environment. While most students are fine, the reality is that some do not make it past the first few weeks. Those who find the situation intolerable might be able to find another place in university accommodation, but some unfortunately decide that uni is not for them and leave within the first term. Thankfully, these cases are in the minority.

Life on a hall corridor is unlike any other situation I have ever come across. There is an immediate bond between students living in the same space, and it comes from the fact that they are experiencing the thrills and spills of student life together. Most people make friends very quickly, and usually by the end of the first week new students are starting to feel settled. Most student corridors are treated as a shared space. Students will usually share bathrooms (although the number of ensuite rooms is increasing) and a kitchen, but even bedrooms are more communal than you might expect. Usually during the daytime, and often at night, bedroom doors are propped open and students will wander in and out of each other's rooms, at ease with sharing their personal space. It is not unusual for students to quickly get used to borrowing each other's possessions and to establish a strong sense of community spirit. Preciousness does not go down well in this environment, and it is best to be as open and tolerant as possible in order to give others the room to behave as they feel comfortable. It is very common for the whole group to spend some time together, either in the kitchen or often in one or two of the bedrooms on the corridor. Anyone with a TV or PlayStation is always popular!

In this environment it is easy to get along with others and have a great time. One of the best things about living in halls is that there is always something going on. With so many people available, it doesn't take a lot of effort to organise something to do, and you will rarely be bored. After just a few weeks of living with this group of people in a hall environment an established code of behaviour will emerge, which the group will adhere to. This unspoken, subconscious human pattern governs how people relate to one another, what is permissible and where the boundaries of the group lie. A social group may not be made up of members of just one corridor or all the members of a single corridor. It is more normal for friendship groups to emerge between several corridors or houses, and for there to be a considerable group of individuals who form a fringe to the group and join in on occasions, but never really become part of the group itself. Breaking this code, or corporate spirit, by doing something out of the established character of the group, or by upsetting one or more of the other members, is to risk conflict.

Are you a peacemaker?

Conflict plays a major part in the life of friends in a uni hall. It is not that it happens all the time, but more that when it does happen it tends to make for a defining moment. All of the groups I have known in halls have had at least one major conflict during a year of living together. With so many different people living together in a fairly small space for so long, it is almost inevitable. It's not a question of whether or not it happens, but what you do about it when it does.

Assuming that you are not right at the heart of the conflict, and are not the person causing a problem for everyone else, you could have a major role in how this time works itself out. When the atmosphere in halls gets a bit tetchy and everyone is upset with everyone else, you could be the peacemaker. What's needed in this kind of situation is someone who will be a friend to everyone concerned and not choose favourites; someone who will try to see everyone else's point of view and try to get people talking to one another; someone who will risk temporary unpopularity to win fairness, encourage the despised and champion the cause of the oppressed. Maybe that someone is you. If you are in direct conflict with a friend in your hall, you will need to take action to sort it out. An apology will go a long way, and often after a few hours of time spent apart you will both feel able to forgive and forget. It's wise to be careful not to judge others and to do your best to accept people as they are and love them for it. Probably the best witness you can give is to love and accept people without prejudice, just as Jesus did. 'My command is this: Love each other as I have loved you. Greater love has no-one than this, that he lay down his life for his friends' (John 15:12–13).

How far will you go?

Closely linked to the question of conflict is that of bound-aries. This is another area of your life in halls that needs some consideration. Just as conflict can be the making or breaking of the community in halls, boundaries can have a lot of impact on you. You will probably go to uni secure in the fact that you have become used to a comfortable set of established boundaries that govern what you will and will not do. As you enter the world of studentdom, prepare for these boundaries to be tested. Uni is a place of excess, and if you are willing to go to extremes, life as a student can take you there. Studentdom has a sliding scale of morality on which you must pick your spot and fight for it. No one will force you to compromise what you believe, or do something you don't want to do, but the pressure will be there. From my experience this pres-sure comes in three forms: peer pressure, beer pressure and tear pressure.

Peer pressure

There was one moment during my time at uni that per-fectly illustrates how your boundaries can be tested when you are with a close group of friends. Living in a house attached to the hall, I had a great time through-out the year and made some good friends. But it wasn't always easy. On this particular night we came home to find our neighbours having a party. We were very unusual in that our neighbours were not from our university, or even normal residents. They were the worst kind of neighbour you can have: students from another university. Not so much neighbours as opposition. Their hall was having some kind of function and we decided to join in. Just as we started to make our way around the fence to gatecrash their celebrations, one of our lads had a bright idea. The opposition had erected a bright white tent in the grounds of their hall to give them more room; the suggestion was made that we all take off our clothes and show them how to party. We hurried back inside and without much hesitation the boys started to strip. I realised I had a choice to make.

This was not my idea of a good night out. It sounded a laugh all right, but what about what I believed? What would Jesus do? I quickly took myself off to the loo to give me time to think. I wanted to go with the guys – I knew it would be a laugh and a major time of bonding. I knew that I had to be a part of this or I'd lose status in the group. I also knew there was no way I was going for a streak around the neighbours' garden! So I hid in the toilet. After a few minutes and a lot of noise, I realised that the guys were looking for me. They hunted all over the house, shouting and banging on doors, but I stayed quiet till they decided to go without me. Needless to say, their impromptu visit next door was a great success. They ran round and round the tent, causing chaos and amusement. Once they got bored with this they took off around our own hall and eventually returned some three hours later, having visited every university hall in the district. The clever ones had remembered to take their trainers. The streak went down in history, partly due to the large number of photographs that appeared everywhere, from the dining room to the student newspaper, over the next few weeks.

As I sat in that smelly toilet, I just didn't know what to do. I desperately wanted to fit in, but I couldn't blow my friendship with Jesus for it. I knew he didn't want me to go and get my kit off. I wanted to take a stand, but I felt so alone. This is peer pressure. You think one thing, your mates think another, and it's a tough job to go with your gut feeling and stay out of trouble. Being strong in a crowd is not easy. That's why it's a good idea to make sure some of your friends feel the same way you do. You can help each other when the heat is on.

Beer pressure

Beer pressure is not unique to studentdom, but nevertheless it is a powerful force when you are living in halls. Everyone knows that students have a reputation for drinking a lot, and it's a fair one because they do. It is very common for a group to have several big nights a week, and for the accepted norm to be something along the lines of emptying every bottle, glass and can in sight. You know as well as I do that when you have had a few sangrias it's not as easy to be clear about how you want to behave, and you can get into a mess fast. How much you drink is up to you, but I would say that the point at which you know you are losing control is the point to have a glass of water and think about what time the next bus leaves for home.

Tear pressure

Whether you cry when you are upset or not is irrelevant. The fact is that when you are feeling low, you are much more likely to want a quick pick-me-up – something to take the blues away. This is tear pressure. The funny thing about life is that it is when we feel really hacked off with the whole deal something naughty floats into our life and we feel seriously tempted to let down our defences. Coincidence? I think not. Be aware that when you are unhappy, for any reason, the natural human response is to look for something to make you happy again. I find at times like these it is better to pick something that God agrees is a good idea, rather than something suggested by the devil.

Not that I have already obtained all this, or have already been made perfect, but I press on to take hold of that for which Christ Jesus took hold of me. Brothers, I do not consider myself yet to have taken hold of it. But one thing I do: Forgetting what is behind and straining towards what is ahead, I press on towards the goal to win the prize for which God has called me heavenwards in Christ Jesus. (Philippians 3:12–13)

Imitating God

You can have a huge influence during your time in halls. A distinctive lifestyle will stick out like a sore thumb in student culture. If you are willing to take a bit of heat, you can make a real difference and will get plenty of opportunities to talk with people about who you are and why you behave as you do. It's not a matter of preaching at people, but simply accepting them as they are, and being a good friend who is always ready to talk and explain what is behind your life. I have believed for a long time that the culture of studentdom is one of the best possible climates to show people the gospel and to see them respond by choosing Jesus for themselves. The close proximity living of halls and houses only adds to this, and the demonstration you give will stay with people a long time. Once uni has finished, most people quickly establish a new pattern of life, and tend to be more closed to new ideas. You may be the only opportunity they ever get to have a relationship with God. That's an awesome responsibility, but also a great privilege and an achievable goal. The Bible shows us that all we have to do is follow Jesus' example: 'Be imitators of God, therefore, as dearly loved children and live a life of love, just as Christ loved us and gave himself up for us as a fragrant offering and sacrifice to God' (Ephesians 5:1–2).

A house or a home?

Living in a university hall and living in a rented student house have many similarities. Much of what has been said about halls can be applied to living in a house with a smaller group of friends. Issues of community, friendship, conflict, boundaries and opportunities to share the gospel are largely the same. The context and nature of life in a house is slightly different, and friendships tend to operate on a deeper level than in the wider relationships facilitated by life in halls. Most students spend at least a year in each type of accommodation, so you are more than likely to experience both.

Finding a house to rent in a student town is surprisingly easy, and the path has been well trodden over the years. The Student Union should offer an accommodation service that will publish a list every year of what is available and how to arrange to view each property. It is worth noting that there tends to be a season for house hunting in which everything can be a bit frantic. This is usually just around the Easter break, when everyone is trying to line up accommodation for the next academic year beginning in September. If there is any way you can beat the rush and get a place sorted before everyone else gets going, it will be worth it. Sometimes you can make a deal with the landlord of a friend you know is moving on, or you can try going through a private agency, but this is likely to be more expensive. All types and sizes of accommodation are available, and the price can vary a lot in the same town, so shop around. Student houses tend to be of a lower standard than you would expect of other rented accommodation, so don't expect a palace. Having said that, student houses can be comparatively cheap to rent, which is to the advantage of the average impoverished student. Although the Student Union carries a list of what accommodation is available, it won't own any of it and usually will not get involved in the process beyond a bit of preliminary marketing.

Once you have found a few options you like the look of, you should arrange to view the properties, and you should strike a deal with the landlord yourself. Usually the landlord will own a handful of properties and have a price in mind. You can try to bargain, particularly if there is a bedroom that is a good deal smaller than the others in the house. There is often a discount to be found here, and you should be careful over the issue of bills and rates. Sometimes these are included and sometimes not, so make sure you check before you sign the contract. The landlord will expect a damage deposit and some rent over the summer break, even if you are not going to live there. Again, look out for hidden charges, take some advice where you need it, and make sure you read carefully anything you sign. You can't be too careful. If you do have any problems or concerns, the Student Union may be able to help you.

Living in a house with a few of your closer friends should be a great experience. This will probably be your first taste of having your own place, and it is a time of learning to look after yourself on a whole new level. Friendships will grow deeper as you learn to live with each other, and many of these relationships will last a long time after the rental contract has expired. For a year or so the people you live with will become your family. You should choose them carefully, looking for friends you know you can be around for long periods of time, and who can be serious as well as good fun. They will be there when you are feeling happy, sad, sociable or in need of time to yourself, and by the end of it they will know you as well as anyone. From my experience this is a time you will look back on as one of the best you have had so far!

5
money and debt

Carl was a funny guy: quiet, lacking in confidence and just a little bit weird. He didn't really click with the other guys on our corridor, and as a result I'm ashamed to say he tended to get picked on. He was immaculately tidy. I mean not a thing was out of place. Ever! He would spend a good part of every day making sure all his possessions were as they should be – that his bed was made and his room was clean. The only problem was that his room was not his own. He had to share it with another guy, Lenny. Lenny was not tidy. Lenny didn't know what the word 'tidy' meant. He liked nothing better than to cover the floor of the room with a layer of abandoned clothes, discarded bedding, newspapers and other trophies of his student existence. He was the guy who always knew where everything was, or so he claimed, until he actually had to find something. Then, unfailingly, he would discover that in actual fact he had lost it. Needless to say, these two room-mates did not hit it off. The more Carl tidied, the more space Lenny had to move into. Over the course of a term, as Lenny's mess became gradually worse, poor Carl found himself spiralling into a pit of despair, otherwise known as a pile of Lenny's used undies. It was bound to end in tears.

Carl's crusade on disorder even extended to his finances. He would make a record of every penny spent and tally this with his income, to make sure he stayed within budget. Under his bed Carl kept a box. In that box, underneath a pile of papers, was a cash tin, which he kept locked. Every evening he would take the cash tin from the box under his bed and open it. He would then empty the contents of his wallet and deposit the coins and notes into the tin, each different denomination of currency in a separate compartment in the tin. He would then lock the box and replace it under his bed, content that his money had been counted, his records adjusted, and all was well with his world. Each morning, Carl would retrieve his cash box, taking out the exact amount of money he needed for that day, being careful to make a note of how much he had borrowed from his personal bank.

One day Carl returned from his lectures to discover a crime had been committed. His world had been turned upside down. More precisely, his safe had been cracked. At first it didn't seem as if anything was wrong; nothing obvious had been moved. It was when Carl came to do his daily accounts that he realised there was a problem. As he opened the cash tin that evening a look of shock spread across his face. He expected to see coins and notes arranged as usual in their own compartments in the tin. What he found that night was that all the coins had been mixed up and the notes rearranged. His coinage was in chaos! It took him a good hour to bring the box back to order and make sure nothing had been taken, which of course it hadn't. The culprits of this heinous crime were never uncovered, but I think it was pretty obvious who had rocked his world. The next day I saw Carl in NatWest bank, opening a student account. There was no way anyone would be able to rearrange his money in there!

Money is a challenging subject. It is difficult to cope with at the best of times, but even more so if you haven't got any. Not all students will take their finances as seriously as Carl, but few will go through student life without giving it some thought at one time or another. There are countless examples of students who have got themselves into all kinds of trouble with their finances during their time at uni, and of course most students in the twenty-first century emerge from studentdom with a serious debt weighing them down before they have done a day's work.

The British Council estimates the average cost of living as a student in London, Oxford or Cambridge as £7,450 per annum, and between £5,150 and £6,700 elsewhere. In 2001 the average student debt, according to the tenth annual Barclays Bank poll, was £5,961, with the total student population in the UK owing nearly £5 billion. It has been claimed that all but 5 per cent of students now have some debt. This was confirmed in December 2000 by the then president of the National Union of Students, Owain James, who commented that figures and experience were showing that student hardship is widespread. Most people now acknowledge that it is a massive problem. Even Tony Blair acknowledged in his Labour Party conference speech in October 2001 that more needed to be done to help students get the education they deserve at a price that does not cripple them for the first decade of their working lives. It was a welcome sight to see him express regret that his party had failed to deliver a fair deal for students during their time in government to that point. Not that it is solely his responsibility. Student debt had been a problem long before Mr Blair swept to power in 1997.

Sources of income

The first thing a student needs to do when considering the state of their finances is to ask: Where does the money come from? There are a number of sources from which students can create an income to cope with the financial demands of student life. Most will use a number of these options to get by during their time at uni.

Parents

Most students benefit from some financial help from their parents while they are studying. When you have accepted a place at uni, and you know what the costs involved will be, you and your parents will be required to fill out a form to ascertain how much money the Local Education Authority believes your parents should contribute to the cost of your education. It is important to note here that although your parents will choose how much they give you, the level of any grants you may receive will be determined by how much the government thinks your parents *should* give you. A few months before you are due to go to uni, it is a very good idea to sit down with your parents, do some sums and have a conversation about how much your life as a student is likely to cost and what they feel they can contribute. This is definitely the best place to start, and will help you begin to budget for yourself.

Local Education Authority

Since 1998 new students have had to pay tuition fees to study at university, whereas these were previously paid for by your local LEA. In 2002, if your parents earn a total income of over £29,784, you will have to pay a full tuition fee of £1,075 for each year of study. If their income is between £20,000 and £29,784 you will have to make a contribution to your tuition fees that is calculated according to the exact amount of their income. If your parents' income is less than £20,000, you will not have to pay tuition fees. LEAs are still able to make grants to supplement the funds of students with special circumstances, such as illness or those coming from very low-income families. If you think you may be eligible, you should talk to your local LEA to find out.

Student loans

You may take out a student loan in each year of your studies, regardless of any other income you may have. You can take as little or as much as you like up to a maximum figure (which is variable by 25 per cent according to the total amount of your parents' income), whether you need it or not. Most students will use their loans to fund their course fees and living costs, although a lot of students get a bit carried away, take more than they need, and squander the excess on social extras. Others will take out a loan and put it in a high interest bank account to earn a little extra money for them, and it is very common for students to use a loan to buy a PC, which is of course a useful tool for their studies as well as a credible alternative to a PlayStation. One of the students on my course at university allegedly managed to persuade two successive girlfriends to take out a loan and lend him the money. The story goes that he terminated the relationships once the money hit his account and never paid them back. It's probably a good idea to make sure you know what you are going to do with the money before you visit the loans clerk! The maximum student loan available in 2002 was £4,815 in London or £3,905 elsewhere and £3,090 living at home.

Banks

All major high street banks provide a service designed specifically for the needs of students. Every autumn, campus branches of the main players in student towns have large posters boasting of the incentives of signing up with their account. The fact is that banks are desperate to secure the accounts of as many students as possible, knowing that in a few years' time those same customers will more than likely be high wage earners, eligible for mortgages, loans, insurance, credit and every other high profit banking service available. Students are just as much the bank's future as they are the future of the workforce for thousands of companies across the world. When you sign up for a student bank account you are likely to receive a reward for your trouble. A free gift of £50 or a personal CD player is typical of the kind of enticement the banks will place in your path. All you have to do is choose where to put your dosh. In reality most students stick with their current bank and upgrade to a student account just before they head to uni. However, you might want to compare interest rates for saving and borrowing, as this is where you may find a major difference in the deals offered. If you are planning on running up a big overdraft, you will want to make sure you get charged minimal interest on this facility. One friend of mine decided to up the stakes a little and play the system. It is taken as read that each student will only take an account with one bank, and usually you have to sign a form to say this is the case. In one day my friend went around all six of the banks offering a deal near the start of his time at uni, and managed to get all the freebies on offer. I don't think they were too happy when they found out! Banks will also offer you credit cards (complete with more freebie incentives) and an overdraft facility. It's all too easy to allow these new spending toys to get out of control, so be careful!

Work

Almost all students earn a bit of extra money by doing some paid work at some point during their student life. It is very common to take full-time work during the summer break, and perhaps during the other holiday times at Christmas and Easter. During a typical summer, working for example as a temp, in a factory, or on a farm, it is quite possible to earn around £2,000. Some students choose to work during term time as well, putting to good use free days, evenings and weekends. Depending on the type of course you are studying, this can be very draining. For a medical student, for example, this kind of work would be almost impossible, as medics are required to spend long days in hospital for their course. Courses that rely less on class time and more on private study make part-time work a more viable option. Shops, bars and restaurants are always looking for young staff, so finding something that suits you should be relatively easy.

Budgeting for student life

Knowing that God is interested in your finances and has taken responsibility for your provision can be a great comfort when things are tough. We have already seen in Chapter 3 that God encourages us not to worry about such things because he promises to look after all that he has made. Going hand in hand with the fact that your money comes from and belongs to God is the responsibility he gives those sharing in his wealth. As he entrusts you with enough for you to live, he expects you to use your money wisely, and to make sure you operate on a basis of what you need, rather than what your latest desire leads you to buy.

In principle, life as a student should fit very nicely with this view on fiscal matters, as students don't tend to have a lot of spare cash, and need what they do have to pay for the essentials. In practice, it doesn't always turn out quite that way, and you could get into a mess by spending what you do have on what you don't need and finding yourself struggling to pay your rent, feed yourself and buy all the books you need. It will not come as a surprise to read that the key to managing your finances is to budget for what you have coming in and what you need to pay out. Once you have made a list of what sources of income are available to you, and one for what your absolute basic needs are, you can add some figures to the budget. It is best to do this first without adding in any contribution from student loans or bank credit. If you need to use these then do so next, but only allow yourself to take what you really need. Keeping your borrowing to a minimum will pay dividends later on; when you graduate you will need all the financial advantages you can get.

Once you have done these sums, hopefully you will have more coming in than going out and you can work out how much per week is left over. This is what you can allow yourself for clothes, music, socialising and any other extras you want. In practice, budgeting may be a lot more complicated than this, and you might want to be more generous than I have suggested. If you are finding financial matters as a student tough, have a word with one of the advisers at the Student Union or uni offices. They will be able to give you confidential help to work out what is best to do, and will have access to hardship funds for those who really need it. Campus branches of banks will also have a student adviser available for you to talk with if you want to.

Studentdom, despite being a place of poverty, is also a place where consumerism rules, much as it does in wider society. Students are by no means immune from the magnetic draw of fashions and fads that will raid any unsuspecting wallet. Materialism, although still a powerful force, is not in the same league as the awesome tag team that make up consumerism. Retail therapy (buying something to make yourself happier) and impulse buying (getting sucked in by a clever ad slogan or a well-placed display stand) are just as apparent in the student world as they are among teenagers and adults. Shopping is a leisure activity for students, and they make for top-notch bargain hunters. There's only one problem with bargains – they still cost money. A bargain is never as cheap as not buying anything at all! Knowing what you need, what you want, and what you will regret buying when you get it home, can be very useful filters through which to squeeze the fruits of your overactive credit card before you sign on the dotted line. Think carefully about what you buy before you flash the fantastic plastic, and you'll do OK.

Carol Midgley, writing in *The Times* in September 2001, recalls how she was shocked by the difficulties some students have in dealing with their finances:

On my very first day at university I made a remarkable discovery. Having spent the evening drinking with my sophisticated new friends, we decided to round off the evening at the chip shop, where I saw a third-year student paying for two bags of chips – total price 60p – *with a cheque.*

One thing that surprises a lot of Christian students is that they are expected to give money away, even though they don't have a lot going spare. Most Christian groups will have regular opportunities for students to give, and churches will still pass around the collection plate, so it seems fair enough when sometimes the odd eyebrow is raised and a cry of 'You cannot be serious!' is heard. That's the thing about God and his cash. He expects us to make sure we don't hold on to all that we have been given for ourselves. I think it's his way of making sure we don't keep our grip too tight on what we don't give away, and don't fall in love with the notes in our wallet. The Bible is very clear: it doesn't matter how much or how little you have, you should give some of it away to help other people out and show God that you love him and that you realise that it is all his anyway. In the Old Testament 10 per cent is given as a useful guideline, but God wants us to consider carefully what we do with all of our money (check out the story of the Rich Young Ruler in Matthew 19 for more on this).

Thinking ahead

One of the most important things to learn about money while you are at uni is that the patterns and standards you set for yourself during this time will be a precedent for the rest of your life. If you get into the habit of spending some, giving some away, and making sure God knows you know it's all his anyway, you won't go far wrong. I know of one guy who started giving while he was at uni, and when he got married soon after he had graduated he and his wife worked out how much they needed to live on and committed to giving away the rest. Their income has increased quite considerably and they now give away over 95 per cent of what they earn. If God can trust you with a little bit, maybe one day he'll trust you with a lot!

6

study and coursework

Theodore Roosevelt said, 'Far and away the best prize life offers is the chance to work hard at work worth doing.' A lot of people would agree with him. The problem for a lot of students is that work can be the last thing on their agenda.

It's easy to forget that being a student is supposed to be primarily about education. Increasing numbers of school leavers in the UK continue their studies by going to university; higher education is becoming the norm. The number of job vacancies advertised which require degree standard education reflects this trend. The perception follows that to do well in life you need a degree, although this is not wholly based on truth. There are a lot of people who have been very successful with little or no formal education, never mind a first from Oxford. Richard Branson's headmaster said to him on the day he left school aged 17 to start his first job, 'Congratulations, Branson. I predict you will either go to prison or become a millionaire.' Most courses at university are of degree standard, although it is possible to study for a diploma or qualification of some other kind. The number of students going on to Master's degrees and beyond is also on the increase as the bar is raised yet higher.

Keeping a sense of perspective while you are at uni is a very good idea. Remembering the reasons why you set out to do something, and what you will achieve if you do, is a helpful tool to making sure you reach your goals. University is no different. However much you enjoy the social side of life in studentdom, and whatever other benefits you gain, the bottom line is this: you are there to work; to make the grade and get yourself a qualification that will give you a great start in your career. If this is true, you must take your studies seriously and do your best to get what you can from this opportunity. That isn't to say you can't have fun along the way, but if you don't scoop the prize at the end of it all, you will have missed the point.

Give it all you've got

Your degree means something. It is not just a piece of paper that tells everyone how clever you are. The work you do week by week, month by month, the skills and knowledge you pick up, and the experience you get working in the field you have chosen, are far more important than what result you get in the end. One should be a reward for the other, and a sign of how accomplished you have become in your specialty. Imagine if medical students were able to take it easy during their five-year course and then fluke a decent grade at the end and become a doctor! When a doctor is diagnosing patients in a busy hospital, what they have learned as they studied will mean a lot more than what their certificate says on graduation day.

Paul was quick, when writing to the church in Colosse, to remind them of the importance of giving their all: 'Whatever you do, work at it with all your heart, as working for the Lord, not for men, since you know that you will receive an inheritance from the Lord as a reward. It is the Lord Christ you are serving' (Colossians 3:23–24).

If you want to do well in your studies and get down to some hard work when you need to, you must see your coursework as valuable. It is not just a means to an end. The facts, knowledge, skills and experience you pick up every day on your course will not only help you in the exam hall during your finals, they will inform you as a person and fuel the work you do every day when you are in the workplace. I remember while I was at school frequently wondering what the things we were learning had to do with real life, and where and when I would ever need these useless facts again. It is much harder to say this of the work you will do at uni. Most students study on courses that relate to what they will do later in life. Even when the link seems tenuous, for example a biochemist who becomes a business manager, the skill level you are expected to operate at in both fields is comparable, and there will be a lot of transferable skills. No university course can fully prepare you for a vocation, no matter how closely they are matched, and no course will fail to equip you in some way for your future career. How well prepared you are for work, through your experiences at uni, varies on a sliding scale between these two extremes. ▶▶16. **career and vocation**

Pace yourself

Most courses at university follow a consistent pattern, which you can rely on to help you get used to the pace you need to work at. Once you know when you are likely to be asked to do a lot of work in a short space of time, and when you will be less busy, it is easier to plan your time accordingly. Each course is different, and not all courses require the same amount of effort to reach a certain grade. If you are on a course that leads to a profession like medicine or law, you can expect to have to work hard most days during the week, and sometimes be at your desk well into the evening. While these courses require a steady rhythm of dedication, more academic courses tend to get progressively more challenging as time goes on. In these courses the first year is often very easy, much less difficult than the A-levels required to get onto the course in the first place. At the beginning of their second year a lot of students have remarked on the noticeable change in pace, as the challenge is stepped up.

This can come as quite a surprise when you have been used to taking it easy. One reason for this sudden leap in course expectations is that assessment, particularly in arts courses, usually only begins from the second year, so the first year is more by way of preparation. Making a good start to the assessed period in this second year will prove to be of great benefit when you are counting every mark as you near the end of your course. Regardless of which course you are on, if you don't have to work hard in your final year, you are either a genius or something has gone badly wrong. I know of very few graduates who will not admit to having had to get their head down and engage their grey matter towards the end of their course to ensure a decent result. As a wise man once said, 'The inevitable always seems to turn up.'

You can help yourself a great deal by finding out as much about your course as possible from the beginning. You should be looking to ask these questions: How is the course assessed, and when will any exams take place? Is the course modular (assessed in small chunks) or does it rely on a final examination? How many lectures, seminars, tutorials and laboratory classes am I expected to attend, and which are compulsory? How many hours of reading am I expected to complete outside of formal class times? Often the best people to help you find the answers to these questions are students in the year above you who are on the same course. They will know what you should expect from the course and be able to advise you on what you need to do. Just remember that everyone is different, so ask a few people to build up a balanced picture.

Armed with this information, you can take an honest look at your studies on a week-by-week basis and work out how much time you are going to need to give to your coursework to do well. You may want to plan out your time a little on a chart or calendar, and write in when essays, reports, a dissertation and all other forms of assessment need to be completed. This will help you work at a steady pace and enable you to know how much time you have in between all that hard graft to relax and enjoy all the other activities available to you as a student.

Time management is not an easy skill to acquire, and student life is not the best environment to succeed. Late nights, heavy drinking and lots of distractions make the discipline of getting some study done that bit harder than it would be elsewhere. One of the keys to working hard when you have to is to see your uni coursework as a job – a job you are required to do well and on time. No one expects you to abandon student culture and work nine to five on essays and lab reports, but having a regular time when you are committed to working on your course will help you build a rhythm that you can stick to.

During the third year of my degree I had to write a long dissertation that was worth a lot of marks towards my final results. I planned to spend time each weekday morning working on this for two or three hours before lunch, and figured that gradually I would get the work done if I stuck to my plan. In practice it was much more difficult than I had thought it would be, and I let the occasional week slip by without making much progress, but overall it definitely helped me to put in the hours I needed to. When it came to the inevitable mad rush to get the paper written, at least I had done the necessary research, even if I had left the writing until the last minute.

Most students find getting out of bed hard, but if you can crack the habit of lying in and employ a little bit of discipline in your student life, you will not only be setting a good foundation for when you have to get up early every day, you will also feel as if you are making a lot of progress in your study. Don't be surprised if your marks go up too! There are two opposing philosophies among students when asked how much work they should do for their course. The first says 'do what you have to do to make it to the end and scrape a decent degree grade', the second says 'do your best and find out what you are capable of'. Unfortunately most students opt for the first of these. I wish I had tried to follow the second.

The most time you'll ever have

Although some university courses can require a lot of work, most students can afford to work about half of their time and do well in their studies. The pace of student life is different both from that of life as a teenager and that of being a young adult beyond university. This is a great opportunity, as you are likely to have more time on your hands in these few years than at any other stage of life. Finding a balance between work, rest and play is essential, but perhaps there are other serious pursuits you can apply yourself to. If you have ever wanted to learn a musical instrument or a foreign language, try a new hobby, or have the time to read a few classics, then this is the place to do it. Not only will you have ample time to give to something new, studentdom is likely to offer you the chance. Sometimes university can feel a little like a holiday camp: so much to do and lots of other people to spend time with. You are unlikely to be bored for very long before you find something to stimulate your mind. ▶▶ 12. the student union and societies

Challenging your worldview

One of the major challenges students face throughout their time at university is that posed by other people's opinions. Particularly when living in halls of residence, you will find that debates on moral, ideological, political and sporting issues are very common, and you will have to get used to being disagreed with. However, it is in the lecture theatre and seminar room that students can feel their worldview is most challenged. For the Christian student, especially in subjects such as medicine, law, philosophy, history, theology and many others, differences of opinion with their classmates and tutors are very common, and often difficult to handle. Traditional Christian values are often scorned in academic circles, forcing those who feel that way to try and stand up for what they believe. The situation is often made more difficult by the fact that tutors will know their subject well, hold very strong opinions and often lack sensitivity when discussing their point of view with anyone who may think differently.

Sometimes this problem can be overcome if the issue in question is presented as a lecture. You can choose simply to listen to what is said and quietly disagree based on your beliefs and values. In a seminar environment this is much more difficult, as you will be asked for your opinion. Disagreeing in written form, in an essay for example, can be even more difficult, as you could risk losing marks if your opinion is deemed wrong, especially if you struggle to back it up with evidence acceptable in your field of study. Simply saying that you believe something often isn't enough.

Unlike school, no one is going to chase you if you fail to turn up to a class or to hand in an important piece of work. Uni is about being responsible for yourself. At the end of the day it is down to you to plan your time, attend your classes and complete the coursework you are set. You are accountable only to yourself. You will be rewarded for what you achieve, but rarely chastised if you don't make the grade. This is an exercise in self-discipline that you will pass if you are determined to do well in your studies and get the degree you deserve. The ball is firmly in your court.

7

revision and exams

Queuing for an exam is a nervous time however much revision you have done. If you are anything like me, you will just want to get on with it. Just before taking one of my uni exams I was pleased to see a friend waiting in line too, so I went over to chat to her. Once I had fought my way through the crowd, I asked Kath how her revision had gone. I knew she was a Christian, but I was really surprised by her answer. She smiled and said, 'I don't revise for exams. I just pray and ask God to help me remember what I need to know.' I was stunned by this revelation and briefly wondered whether I should follow Kath's method for the other exams I was due to take. But somehow I was sure that it was down to me to put in the hard work.

Exams form part of most university courses. It is highly likely that at some stage during your studies you will have to sit an exam. The importance placed on exams varies from course to course: some will have exams all the way through and others exams at the end of the course. The percentage of your final grade that rests on exams will also vary, but it is probable that you will need to perform well in exams to get the grades you are hoping for. In recent years the modular system of assessment has become more popular, allowing some of the pressure of exams to be released by testing students at regular intervals. One of the famous images of university life is that of 'Finals' exams at the end of a three year course, where everything is at stake and all the student has learned is tested over a few short days.

In most cases that system has now gone. Modules are self-contained study units of about twelve weeks' learning. There is likely to be some assessed coursework along the way, and at the end of the module there will be an exam to test what you have learned. There are two main benefits to this system, which make it fairer for those who are not suited to big exams and for anyone who has an off day. First, the pressure and expectation around exams is dissipated so that students are not so churned up about success or failure in two or three exams. Second, should a student do badly in one of these modular tests there is quite often an opportunity to retake the exam and do better the second time around. For those who have always feared exams this is good news, as the exams you do have to take are smaller, and fewer course marks depend on them. The downside is that there are more of them!

Some courses still hold to the older system of big exams at the end of the year. It's important to find out as early as you can how your course is assessed so that you can prepare properly. You may even want to know about this kind of thing before you commit yourself to the course in the first place.

Playing to your strengths

It's not all bad news though. Some people love exams! They prefer to relax for the rest of the time and cram for a few days before exam day to make sure they know their stuff. Degree courses tend to discourage this kind of approach as they look for consistency and commitment to the course, but exams still hold a lot of weight, so there is something to be gained for all types of student. Courses are continually being adapted to try and make them as fair as possible when it comes to assessment. Some students prefer exams and others prefer course-work. Most courses are now a blend of the two, and tend to steer clear of any one piece of assessment carrying too many marks to ensure that you don't either blow it all or fluke it on one day. Personally, I quite liked exams because I felt that as long as I had prepared, I could cope when it came to whatever was on the question paper.

Planning to revise

I cannot over-emphasise the need for you to plan when it comes to exams. You can't just turn up on the day and wing it, however hard you pray. During exam times many students will have back-to-back exams for several days, so last-minute revision can be a bad option too. The only way to do well and make sure you do not crack under the pressure is to put the hours in from the start and plan well ahead. Your faculty will know when exams are to take place from the beginning of each year of your studies, so there is no excuse for not knowing when they will come up. In any case, nearer the time of each exam they will be well advertised and your tutors will make sure you know about them in plenty of time.

As you start a unit of study it is a good idea to find out how it is assessed, what proportion of the marks is based on exams, and when those exams are likely to be. If the course is taught well, there should be some provision towards the end of the teaching time to review what you have learned and help you organise your revision.

Very few people do well in exams without revising what they have learned and boiling down their knowledge to a core that they can remember without notes. Revision is very much a short-term memory technique, which is why some people question assessment by exams in the first place. Often students will struggle to remember what they revised just a few weeks after the exam, the whole purpose of the revision having been to pass the exam, not to take that knowledge on into life with them. However, knowing that revision is about short-term memory can be helpful. For the majority of people revision is most effective near to the time of the exam they are revising for. It is good to get some rest, maybe a day immediately before the exam, but you should generally aim to revise in the days leading up to the exam, and concentrate your work on that task alone. This can be complicated if you have several exams to face over a period of a few days, but nevertheless the theory is the same.

The first thing you must do when planning your revision is to look over all the work the course has covered and divide it into topics so that you can revise in small blocks. The human memory is a bit like a tree. It works in branches rather than being a random collection of facts and memories. From the trunk you can access a few branches, which then lead to more branches and so on. To help you revise, it is a good idea to divide up your work into 'branches' so that you do not confuse yourself with trying to remember everything as a whole. You need to think about how long it would take you to revise each of these units. Perhaps a day or half a day would be a good amount of time to spend on each, depending on how much there is to revise. Once you have some structure to your revision, you can work out when you will look at each unit. Working backwards from the day of the exam, allowing for some rest to let your brain recover, calculate how many days of revision you will need to cover all you have learned in the course. You may find it helpful to cover each unit more than once, gradually boiling down what you know into a smaller number of key components that you find it easy to remember. Your experience in GCSEs and A-levels will help you work out how you revise best.

Most students find it helpful to make notes of some kind as they revise, to help them in this process of focusing their revision on a few key points. Studies have proved that writing something down can help you to remember it later on. This is especially helpful if your original notes are typed. You are much more likely to remember something you have written yourself than if you just read from a typed sheet. It is all too easy to stare at a page for a few hours, or even read most of a book, and not take in what is written in front of you. Forcing yourself to make notes will help you engage with the material and seriously increase your chances of remembering what you need to.

Keeping your notes as brief as possible is a good idea, as you can only remember so much. Writing a book of revision notes will not help you remember very much, and will only take up more of your precious revision time. Trying to get each unit onto one sheet of paper may be a helpful idea, although if you are tempted to go and buy an A1 pad just to cram it all in, consider allowing yourself another piece of A4. Some people find it helpful to make revision cards, which they can use to trigger their memory as they revise. By using each card to record a single idea, diagram, picture, function, phrase or quote you can break down your revision into very small units, which can be easier to remember in the exam hall.

How you revise is really a matter of personal choice. There is no one way that is guaranteed to work. Courses vary hugely and every student has a different method of revision that they know works for them. The ideas above are simply a starting point, mainly to emphasise the need to plan ahead and to go with whatever works for you. There are two key techniques that everyone should use to increase their effectiveness in revision, no matter what the subject or what other techniques they choose to employ. They are rest and reward.

Rest

However great the pressure, however little time there is to go before the exam, you must rest! Your brain will only work at full power for a short time before it goes into decline and eventually shuts down all together. Think of it like a battery; it only has a limited time that you can run it without a recharge. You should make sure you rest in two different ways. First, take some time to rest before and after each exam to let your body recover. Taking exams is stressful and places strain on your body and mind. Make sure you get a few hours off the day before the exam and don't plan anything for immediately afterwards! Second, you should aim to take regular breaks as you study, to optimise your memory retention. Researchers have found that a break of 10 to 15 minutes every hour helps most students to get the best out of the remaining time. I used this kind of work/rest pattern during my time at uni and found it really helpful. You might think this is a lot, but believe me it works! Make sure when you take this kind of break that you get up from your desk, move away from your work space and stretch your legs. You might like to get a drink or a snack to keep you going and energise your mind! At lunchtime take a longer break of perhaps an hour, and again make sure you get away from your work and rest your mind. You may find that some light exercise helps to refresh you and motivate you for the afternoon.

If you have planned properly you should not need to work through the evening to revise properly. Make sure you get some time off to relax, be with your friends, go to the gym, or whatever you want to do. Get some 'me time' as the Americans like to say. If you are a night bird and prefer to work later on in the day, substitute the evening for the morning or afternoon and take some rest time then instead. A good rule of thumb is to divide the day into three equal parts of morning, afternoon and evening, and make sure you only work during two of these three parts. If you burn the candle at both ends and work all day every day you will run out of steam very quickly and minimise your chances of remembering what you need to.

Reward

Rest and reward are closely linked. Both aim to help you work at your best and motivate you to keep going. Rest is one form of reward but there are others. Rewarding yourself for studying hard can be a great way of getting the job done. You might like to get something special for lunch, plan an evening you will enjoy, or dream up some other reward that you can have when you complete part of your revision. Making your rest time as enjoyable as possible will help you work hard when you need to. If you are in a relationship you may like to think about how you can help each other to revise properly. Revising together is a tempting prospect but does it really maximise your exam performance? Planning to spend time together when you have both reached your goals can be a good way of making sure you get the work done and rewarding yourself when you have finished. Trying to help your partner do as well as they can by protecting their study time is the best way of looking after them during this time.

If you have planned ahead, prepared well and taken some time to rest, you should be able to approach your exams with confidence. You can only do your best, so you should not worry too much about what will happen but trust yourself to do well. If you are in the habit of praying, taking a few minutes to ask God to help you do your best might be a good idea before you go into the exam room. Nerves can be useful to help you concentrate and take the task seriously, but allowing yourself to get too worked up will not help. If you suffer badly from this kind of apprehension, try using some relaxation techniques before and during the exam. There are some very useful techniques that you can use, normally based on breathing.

What is the worst that can happen? By way of reassurance I'll tell you what happened to me during a big exam while I was at uni. I had studied hard, revised well and even taken some time out to relax the day before. It was a big exam, contributing heavily to the final result of my degree, and I wasn't about to take it lightly. I was confident and ready to perform. My mind was focused on the task. Nothing could stop me doing well in this exam. As I took my seat in the large exam hall I felt good, even excited, about getting on with writing my answers to the paper. The invigilators brought around the question papers and the exam began. I was pleasantly surprised that the questions on the paper looked quite easy, and I began to write my first answer. An hour or so passed and I felt I was doing well, on time and on course for a good result. And then it all went wrong ...

At first I didn't notice – I was too busy creating my next great sentence. Then I spotted I had a problem. My exam paper was changing colour and my hand was covered in a sticky red liquid. At first I thought my pen must be leaking, and then, realising that its ink was blue, it began to dawn on me what was happening. I was having a nosebleed. A big one, with flow to match the most prolific of volcanoes. Within seconds the desk was awash, and both question and answer papers were ruined. Realising I needed help, I put up one bloodied hand to gain the attention of the nearest invigilator. By this time the flow had reached the floor and fellow students were starting to move away. Help arrived and then left again to get some tissues. I was trying hard not to make too much noise, but already quite a commotion had broken out. The invigilator returned with tissues, looking more than a bit flustered by this unexpected event. I was still struggling to stop the problem, not helped by the girl on my left who was seemingly intent on breaking my neck by tipping my head back at an impossible angle. I managed to fight her off and stop the outpouring, but it was too late to save my answer paper, and the desk was unusable. I was escorted from the room, still clutching half a box of tissues and a blood-stained bic. Needless to say I had to re-sit the exam a few days later. This time I prayed for God to calm my nerves *and* help me not to bleed. I passed the exam . . . just.

As I write this I pray you will be spared that kind of exam nightmare. Good luck. Your best is all anyone can ask of you.

8

friends and community

There is one thing I will never forget about my time at university. It's not the course or the social life; not the sport, the food or the exams. I will never forget the day that Georgie died. Six of us lived on a corridor, not the best of friends, but mates all the same. Sometimes we spent time together, at other times we did our own thing. One day I was woken up at 5 a.m. by a knock on the door and a voice asking me to come to the kitchen. We assembled there to be told that one of the girls who lived with us had died in an accident. It was a horrible day that none of us will ever forget.

Shock waves went around the hall as the news spread. No one knew quite what to do with themselves, and no one knew what to say. I decided to go in to uni and attend the lectures I had that day. I figured I would try and carry on as normal and keep my mind on other things. I felt as if my insides had been ripped out – I was gutted. Having struggled through those few hours at uni I made my way home, not looking forward to the atmosphere back in the hall. Walking back to my room was weird; no one was around. There was none of the usual activity and banter. When I stepped through the door to my corridor I saw a friend waiting for me. Al had heard what had happened and came to see if I was OK. He hadn't worried about what he had to do that day, but had come miles out of his way to sit outside my room and wait until I came home. I can't remember ever needing to see a friend more than I did in that moment. He didn't stay long; just long enough to make a cup of tea, listen to me for a few minutes and pray. I will never forget how much that meant to me. That is what friendship is all about. Friends are the people who are always there, no matter what. They are those who will drop everything to come and see you when you need them most.

David and Jonathan

David, who was to become the king of Israel, had a friend like that. His name was Jonathan. David and Jonathan were best mates. They did everything together and would do anything for one another. Even when it got as tough as it gets, Jonathan was there for David. Part of their story is told in the Bible, in 1 Samuel 20. David was on the run. The king of Israel was trying to kill him because he felt humiliated by David's success against the giant, Goliath, and by the way God favoured David. David had escaped and was hiding when he found Jonathan and they talked together. David asked Jonathan in desperation, 'What have I done? What is my crime?' and Jonathan assured him by replying, 'You are not going to die!' The two friends talked together some more and Jonathan pledged to David, 'Whatever you want me to do, I'll do for you.' Finally they made a covenant of friendship together to show how much their friendship meant to them:

> David got up from the south side [of the stone] and bowed down before Jonathan three times, with his face to the ground. Then they kissed each other and wept together – but David wept the most. Jonathan said to David, 'Go in peace, for we have sworn friendship with each other in the name of the Lord, saying, "The Lord is witness between you and me, and between your descendants and my descendants for ever."' (1 Samuel 20:41–42)

These guys were willing to do anything for each other. They were such close friends that they even felt able to cry with each other. That's a pretty difficult thing for any man to do! And there is a twist to their story that makes it all the more amazing. Saul, the man trying to kill David and the ruling king of Israel, was Jonathan's father. Jonathan was so deeply committed to David that he was even willing to risk his own life, and his relationship with his dad, for his friend. Now that's friendship.

A couple of chapters previous to this part of the story, we see the key to David and Jonathan's friendship. It's the same factor that is at the bottom of all relationships that mean something: love. 'After David had finished talking with Saul, Jonathan became one in spirit with David, and he loved him as himself' (1 Samuel 18:1). Jonathan loved David as himself! Not nearly as *much* as himself. He loved him *as* himself. He was willing to put David first. Even above his own needs.

This is the key to friendship and a lesson we can all learn from. If we want to be the best friend we can, we have to stop seeing friends as our ticket to happiness and fulfilment, and ask ourselves how we can be theirs. John F. Kennedy, in his famous inaugural speech, said, 'Ask not what your country can do for you. Ask what you can do for your country.' We need to address that same mentality to our friendships. The question is not what we can get out of our friends but what we can give to them.

Real friendship

This is a very hard thing to achieve at university. We all desire to have the kind of deep and meaningful friendship that David and Jonathan had, but it is much harder to achieve in practice than in theory. You could easily have many friends at uni and yet still feel a deep sense of loneliness and fear. Mother Teresa once said that the greatest problem she had come across was not any kind of disease, but helping those who felt alone. Loneliness is very common at uni, even though there are so many people around all the time. The friendship issue is not one of quantity but one of quality. The circle of friendship at uni is wide. It includes people from very different backgrounds and people with very different ideas. This is a good thing, as it is unhealthy to have friendships only with those who are the same as you. The key is to make friends with people you have the ability to go deeper with over time. You need to find some mates who will get under the surface and begin to uncover even the really nasty bits about you. This kind of friend is like gold dust.

Everyone needs friends. Even Jesus needed a group of people around him that he could trust, talk to and share his life with, in the good times and the bad. These were the guys who were there when Jesus went to a wedding. They were holding the grave clothes when he raised a friend from the dead. They were there when he was arrested, and they stood under his cross when the Romans took his life. He loved them and they loved him. They wept together, talked together, prayed together and ate together. In fact, they did everything you would expect in spending three years together. They were his friends.

Greater love has no-one than this, that he lay down his life for his friends. You are my friends if you do what I command. I no longer call you servants, because a servant does not know his master's business. Instead, I have called you friends, for everything that I learned from my Father I have made known to you. (John 15:13–15)

Who are your friends?

Pause now and think of your friends. Who are they? How well do you know each other? Is there anything you wouldn't do for each other? Are there limits to your friendship? Can you be open and honest with each other about how you are feeling? You might like to make a decision now that you will go deeper with your friends; that you will put them first and invest in their lives because you want the best for them.

I find it helpful when thinking about how I can be a better friend to think about what I call priority relationships. You can't be best friends with everyone, and you can't spread your time so thinly that you never really spend any time with anyone. Priority relationships are those people closest to you, those you want to spend the most meaningful time with; they are your priority. By identifying these people you can look to invest time and energy into them and deepen your relationship. This doesn't mean that you won't spend time with other people, but just that you are being more proactive about your friendships. I tend to think about this for the whole of my life, so my priority relationships would be: my wife, my mum and dad, my brother, my grandmother, the guys I work with, and my two best mates. That's it. No more than a handful of people.

You could say that for Jesus his priority relationships were with his disciples. Ten to twelve people is a good number to bear in mind. Much more than this and you will be struggling to spend meaningful time with them all on a regular basis. These are the people who love you no matter what, will be there if you need them, at any cost, and who know you are not perfect all the time. They will forgive you when you stuff it up. They know the real you, and still think you are great. When you think about who these people may be for you, probably only a few of them will be friends from uni. If you have never discussed your friendship with these people, I suggest you subtly raise the subject at some point and clarify your expectations. It's good for you to know that you have this kind of friendship with one or two key people whom you can rely on no matter what.

I have believed for a long time that friendship is God's currency, and that it is the basic building block for community between human beings. Not only do we find happiness, love, commitment and forgiveness in our friendships, we also have a few people around us who can look after us when we need it and make sure we don't go off the rails. In my experience when we have been doing something we shouldn't have been doing, and we know we have strayed from what our life is about, it is our friends who correct us and help us get back on track. It is pretty rare these days for God to send a lightning bolt to sort us out when we need a little help in our lives. He tends to use our friends to help us live for him and behave as we should. It's no coincidence that God uses love to remind us of how much he loves us, how much we love him and what that means in terms of the way we choose to live.

The enemy of this kind of lifestyle is the secret. The more we can share with those close to us, the more likely we are to be living with integrity. If there are things in our lives that only we know about, things that have become secrets, it is more than likely that those things are or will be a problem at some point. I have been challenged recently to share more of how I feel with people around me and have been amazed at how much difference this simple vulnerability has made. Just talking with people can be a huge release, even if they have no answers to offer you.

Friends for life

You will also have a wider friendship group at uni with whom you will not be so intimate. These friends are important too. One of the great things about student life is the opportunity it affords you to get to know a wide range of people and spend time with them regularly through each week. Studentdom is a place where friendships that are given time and energy will flourish and become very meaningful. Work at your friendships and they will bring you great rewards.

There are increasing numbers of international students attending UK universities. These young men and women have travelled many thousands of miles to be educated in the UK and can feel very isolated and alone. Particularly at the beginning of their visit, a lot of international students struggle to make friends, not least because of their limited knowledge of English. It can be very frightening and demoralising to be so far away from home in a new and very different culture. Often internationals will only spend time with each other as British students make little effort to get to know them. Perhaps there are some international students on your course or living nearby whom you can get to know? Not only will you be helping them, but you will be enriched by the differences in culture and their perspectives on life.

Friendship is also a powerful means of spreading the gospel. Much as I am sure he appreciates the efforts of street evangelists, mission teams, stadium events and TV God slots, it is friendship that really cuts the missionary mustard. More people come to know Jesus for themselves through the example, testimony and guidance of a friend than through any other route. It is essential to spend time with people who think the same as we do so that we can be encouraged and cared for, but equally important is to spend meaningful time with those who do not share our beliefs.

I have known a lot of Christians who, during their time at college, have gone one of two routes and struggled to connect their faith with reality. Either they have lived in some kind of Christian subculture, a faith ghetto, where their only friends are Christians and they hide from the reality of student life, or they dive in with two feet to all uni has to offer, losing touch with Christian friends and finding they are tempted beyond belief to compromise their friendship with Jesus. Neither of these extreme approaches is really an option, and thankfully I increasingly find Christian students who have a reliable bunch of Christian and non-Christian friends to share their student life with. Those who really impress me are the ones who have taken down the walls and live a seamless life with a mix of friends of all types. They are just a friend to their mates, some of whom know God for themselves. That's the golden standard if you want to make a real difference in friendship to those around you.

If you have seen the film *Good Will Hunting*, you will remember the scene in which Will, played by Matt Damon, and his best friend Chuckie, played by Ben Affleck, discuss their future while taking a break from their work on a building site. Chuckie challenges Will to make the most of his extraordinary talent, appalled by the prospect of him being in the same place in 20 years' time. He is willing even to lose his friend if it means that Will can have the opportunity to do well.

Friendship means being prepared to give up everything, even the friendship itself, for the sake of the other person. Uni will give you a great opportunity to make friends with loads of people, some of whom you may know for the rest of your life. Will you take the chance to get to know people as well as you can, using the time student life provides to be the best friend they know?

9

relationships and sexuality

Sharing a room in my first year at uni was fun. My room-mate (let's call him Tim) and I quickly became good mates and enjoyed spending time together. Our similar interests gave us plenty to talk about and we were able to laugh about anything and everything. At first the thought of sharing a room with someone for a year was daunting. Most people would rather have some space to themselves, and I was no different. Despite our reservations, we quickly got used to each other and began to enjoy the experience. Then Tim got a girlfriend. At first things were fine – Tim was around less and sometimes his new girlfriend came over to visit. After a short while Tim started not to come back to our room overnight (they weren't Christians). I didn't have a problem with that at all – if anything it was quite nice to have the place to myself sometimes – but I did have something to say about it when Tim was safely installed in his bed and his girlfriend decided to pay a return visit!

Studentdom is a liberal society with few rules and a low morality threshold. Students are exposed to, and usually part of, a culture that lives by the code of freedom. You are free to do what you want, any old time. Nowhere is this more evident than in the area of sexuality. Sex is a dominant force in uni life. When you consider the inhabitants of studentdom this is no surprise. Thousands of young people are entering their sexual prime, mixed with a good measure of alcohol and a twist of new-found liberation, and that's a fairly potent cocktail. Right from the word 'go' most of the entertainment to be found on campus plays off the slick partnership of alcohol and sex. Don't get me wrong – you are unlikely to come across a strip show or a movie night featuring the latest porno, but the availability and willingness of a multitude of sexual partners is all too obvious. Invariably the stereotype is proved true: students have sex on the brain.

In every part of student life there are extremes and norms. In terms of sexuality it is extreme to suggest that every night of the week, every student on every campus is sleeping in a different bed. Of course there are a good number of students who choose to sleep around, but there are a fair few who don't live that way. Sometimes this is because they want to take a little more care when it comes to sex; for others perhaps they just haven't landed a catch yet. While it is dangerous to make generalisations, when it comes to sexuality studentdom is as open and permissive a society as you will find. Sex is a very real issue for students, and unfortunately it is one where the current of popular student culture seems to predominantly flow in only one direction. The perception on most campuses is that if you are not looking to get laid, there is something wrong with you. At many student events if you do not leave with a sexual partner by your side it can feel as though you have somehow failed. Even if you have decided not to jump into bed with the first person you meet, it is easy to lose your resolve after a few short weeks and do something you'd rather you hadn't. Uni life makes it very easy to form casual relationships, often with more than one person, sleep with them if you want to, all the time steering clear of any kind of commitment.

A lot of my friends while I was at uni would have sex with someone simply because they were bored, or even worse, because they missed their partner from their home town. For Christians and others who choose to stay out of sexual relationships, it is very easy to get into a friendship with someone you are attracted to, maybe even another Christian, and for that friendship to quickly change into an exclusive relationship where sex is a massive temptation.

God created sex

God is very serious about sex. He did not create it simply

as a means by which we could produce children, or as a test for us to pass and prove how much we love him. Sex is a gift from God, designed for our pleasure. He created us as sexual beings. The urges, passions and desires we all have are natural and very much part of who he has made us to be, and it is in the way that we choose to behave that we can glorify him:

> For this reason a man will leave his father and mother and be united to his wife, and they will become one flesh. The man and his wife were both naked, and they felt no shame. (Genesis 2:24–25)

When God created Adam and Eve, he told them how it was to be: men and women should be united, becoming one flesh. Notice that in this part of the creation story the man and his wife were naked, and they were not ashamed. Their sexuality was on display; they and God were proud of this part of humanity and wanted to celebrate together. This verse is often used in the marriage ceremony to remind us that God is the one who first came up with the idea of a man and a woman joining together in the act we call sex.

Sex is a complicated thing. God has told us that the conditions must be just right, and that he thinks sex is best when part of something more than a one night stand. Unlike many Hollywood scenes, it is not a case of boy meets girl and within 20 seconds boy and girl are in bed in a steamy scene. The Bible tells us that God has created sex in the context of a lifelong relationship between one man and one woman. Those are the perfect conditions – the maker's instructions if you like. Sex in any other context is not on. The New Testament is particularly clear on this: 'Flee from sexual immorality . . .' (1 Corinthians 6:18).

It is clear that our sexuality comes from God. By this I do not mean what sexual orientation we have, but the fact that sexuality (the expression of being a man or a woman) is part of being human. It is how he has created us. Our sexuality is expressed through friendship as well as sexual relationships. It influences our character, our taste, the way we dress, what we do and don't like, how we behave, how we play sports, how we decorate where we live, how we show love and what we choose to do for entertainment. Sexuality is not something we can turn on or off. We do not change when we become aroused; this is simply a further expression of our sexuality. All of this means that sexuality can be expressed in ways other than sexual intercourse. For many young men and women it seems as though the only way that their sexuality shows itself, particularly in student culture, is by them going to bed with someone they have just met. It was never meant to be that way.

This also means that it is OK to be single. Our culture scorns singleness as some kind of failure, and single people are often looked upon as 'sad'. In student culture this is not so obvious, as there are lots of people who are not in a relationship, but for those who are looking for a long-term relationship the pressure of being single for a long time can be intense. Especially in the Christian scene, it can feel as though you have in some way not made the grade if you are not in a couple by the time you have graduated.

Homosexuality

The majority of university students are heterosexual and normally choose to stick to one partner at a time, even if they do change them quite frequently. However, there are a significant number of students who are gay or bisexual. Being gay is very acceptable in student culture, probably more so than in mainstream society. Studentdom encourages experimentation, and many students will have first-time experiences while they are in halls during their first year. Where homosexual feelings have been suppressed or rejected at home, they often emerge when the student is liberated by the tolerance student culture provides. Student Unions are very likely to put on gay and bisexual nights, and there will usually be a society (often called LGB, for lesbian, gay and bisexual) that anyone is free to join to get involved in gay events and spend time with other gay people. Christian groups that do little to understand or build bridges with the gay community at university often risk marginalising a lot of their fellow students. In turn Student Unions have been known to bring motions against Christian groups for refusing to accept gay members and for declaring homosexuality to be wrong. This is an issue that the whole of the church will have to do a lot more to engage with, and nowhere is this more obviously needed than in the student world. It is essential that Christians be seen first to love and accept those around them and then to discuss the issues where opinion is divided. The Bible is clear that God did not intend same-sex relationships when he created human beings. However, homosexuality is a reality in student life, and while Christians must stand for biblical principles, this has to be done in the context of friendship, humility and grace. ▶▶12. **The Student Union and Societies**

Romance isn't dead

University is a great place to build a relationship with a boyfriend or girlfriend. Having so much time to spend together and a lot of activities to get involved in is a great foundation for getting to know each other really well. Romancing at uni needn't be expensive – even a hall bedroom can be converted into a candlelit restaurant with a bit of effort. My friend Pete decided to do just that on Valentine's Day one year. Wanting to surprise his girlfriend, Miri, he bought 100 tea-lights and arranged them around his room to create a romantic effect. Miri was thrilled that he had gone to so much trouble and they sat down to tuck into the fruit salad she had prepared for them to eat together. With the heat of all the candles the room was getting hot, so Pete went to open the window and let in some air. As a breeze entered the room it fanned the flames and before Pete could sit down his carpet was on fire. They stamped out the flames, but were unable to prevent the carpet being damaged, and Pete had to pay £132 to have it repaired. Thankfully this didn't put Miri off, and they married between their finals and graduation and are now setting more of the world ablaze as they start their careers!

Like Pete and Miri, a lot of couples meet while they are studying at the same uni and go on to get married. Each year I get invited to four or five weddings of couples who have met in this way. Most students will have a relationship of some kind while they are at uni, and in my experience from talking to many students, most will struggle at some time in their relationship. Uni is a great place to get to know each other, but couples often have problems deepening their relationship over time while avoiding going too far in their physical relationship. I have found that one key to managing this balance is to spend plenty of time together as part of a larger group. This will help you as a couple to interact with each other and the group on a deeper level and provide some much needed breathing space in terms of your personal intimacy. Often a couple will behave differently in public to how they do in private, which can lead to tension between them, but it will help them to understand more about each other and be more tolerant of each other's differences.

Another distinct advantage of being part of a group at

uni is that this will provide plenty of friends with whom you can be honest about how things are going in your relationship. Having a few friends around who will ask the difficult questions and give you some advice when you need it is essential if the relationship is to go the distance. A lot of couples at uni get too serious too soon and become detached from their friends in a matter of weeks. This is bound to lead to problems, not least if it all goes wrong, as you may find you have few friends to pick up the pieces. Much better to take it slowly, get to know each other properly, spend plenty of time with your other friends, and stay out of trouble.

Home is where the heart is

It is very common for students to have a boyfriend or girlfriend at home. Being a student will usually be the first time they have been away from their partner for a long period of time, and suddenly having a long distance relationship can be very difficult. I have known a lot of couples that have been rock solid before one of them went to uni and within a few short months their relationship is in tatters. With some relationships this is a natural part of growing up, and it is right for the relationship to come to an end. With others, if a little more care had been taken the relationship could have perhaps survived this traumatic time. It always seems as though the change is most difficult for the person left at home, as they have none of the fun of being in a new place and are more than likely to spend a good part of their time wondering what their partner is up to. Communication is the key.

If you are in this situation you need to have a long, frank conversation before you go off to uni and make sure you keep talking all the way through. Talking about your expectations for the relationship through this change will help you both to feel more comfortable with what you are going through and build the trust between you. If one of you expects more than the other you must try to resolve the issue before you leave for Freshers Week. While you are away you must both try to tell each other how you feel, and always check your actions through the filter of putting the other person first. Girls particularly should be aware that a guy left at home will feel very jealous if they give him an excuse. Plenty of visits and a healthy dose of consideration should help you get through the first few months, and hopefully you will get used to the situation and find a way for the relationship to flourish while you are apart.

Going out with a non-Christian

If there is one question I am always asked when it comes to relationships at uni it is this: should Christians go out with non-Christians? I could quote Bible verses left, right and centre, and I know that some Christians have very strong opinions on this subject. It is a big issue and a lot of Christian students find themselves in a situation where they have to make a choice. The golden rule in all relationships is to consider whether there is any possibility you will marry this person. If that is never going to happen, should you be in a relationship with them in the first place? I'm not saying that you need a ring on your finger in the first week, but there should at least be a chance that you could be with this person for good. If not, you are just messing around and it's time to call it a day. Most Christians I know have decided that they want to marry someone with the same beliefs as them. On this basis the majority of them would not go out with a non-Christian because they know they will never marry them. I have known a few people who have become Christians through a relationship, but a lot more don't. Paul advises in 1 Corinthians 7:39 and 2 Corinthians 6:14–15 against relationships with non-Christians. You have to think about the pressure such a relationship will put on you both. Are you going to lead your partner closer to God, or are they going to lead you further away?

A perfect 10?

When considering any kind of relationship, it is a good idea to think ahead a bit and weigh up what you are looking for in a suitable partner. Some people like to be very specific and others are more general, preferring to fill in the details when they meet someone. Towards the end of my time at uni I began to think about this more seriously and found it very helpful in how I looked at relationships. I realised that up until that point I had relied almost entirely on my feelings to decide whether or not I liked a girl. Once I began to think about what kind of person I would like to be with, I realised where a few previous relationships had gone wrong. I thought of a short list of what I was looking for in the future Mrs Stuart and found it a lot easier to steer clear of trouble after that. Top of the list was someone I could pray with, someone who loved music and movies, someone who was a bit sporty, someone who wanted to see the world, and someone who wanted me to be me. Of course I also had a few more visual requirements, but I think I'll keep those to myself. If you think it would be helpful for you to spend some time thinking about who you would like to be with, I would encourage you to do that now and to use that list to help you avoid one-off encounters and find someone you are likely to be able to build a deeper relationship with.

Searching for purity

God asks us simply to have purity in the way we behave. From our thought life to where we put our hands, the standards are the same. It's easy to go out at uni looking for a casual snog or more. It's easy to flirt with people and lead them on. It's easy to end up in bed with someone you hardly know. Thousands of students do that stuff all the time. I want to challenge you to live differently; to think before you act; to go for the very best, and to know that is what God wants for you too. Paul reminds the church in Ephesus what they have to live up to:

> So I tell you this, and insist on it in the Lord, that you must no longer live as the Gentiles do, in the futility of their thinking. They are darkened in their understanding and separated from the life of God because of the ignorance that is in them due to the hardening of their hearts. Having lost all sensitivity, they have given themselves over to sensuality so as to indulge in every kind of impurity, with a continual lust for more. You, however, did not come to know Christ that way. Surely you heard of him and were taught in him in accordance with the truth that is in Jesus. You were taught, with regard to your former way of life, to put off your old self, which is being corrupted by its deceitful desires; to be made new in the attitude of your minds; and to put on the new self, created to be like God in true righteousness and holiness. (Ephesians 4:17–24)

If you can do that, and remain humble enough not to judge others who don't find it so easy, you will be doing very well. A lot better than I did . . .

10

eating and drinking

M eeting your friends in the uni bar after a lecture is not unusual practice for the average student. Pete and I lived in the same house, and as we finished at the same time that day, it seemed natural to get together for a pint after a hard hour's learning. We met in the bar as we had done many times before and ordered a cheap pint each. The bar was half full, as was usual for a week-day afternoon, and we settled into a corner to enjoy our drink and have a chat.

For some reason, that day we stayed in the bar longer than we normally would have, chatting to others who came in and enjoying the atmosphere. One pint turned into two, and then three, and then four or five. Neither of us had had much to eat and we soon realised that the beer was having its effect and it was probably time to leave. We said our goodbyes to our mates and made for the door, trying hard to remember where we had left our bikes. Once we had located the bikes we hopped on them, rode across the park and made for home.

We chatted and laughed as we cycled down the middle of the streets, and giggled as we swayed in the wind. As we neared home on quieter roads I pulled ahead, our house looming in the middle distance. Then there was a thud, and a second or so later a crash, as Pete and his bike met with the road at the wrong angle. I stopped my bike and turned to look, as Pete struggled to his feet, rubbed his knee and sucked the side of his hand, which had taken the brunt of the blow. As I realised what had happened, and that Pete was OK save a few minor injuries, I began to laugh. In this empty road there was only one obstacle we had to avoid in order to make it home safely. Pete had managed to hit a parked car at full speed and bounce off to face the wrath of the tarmac.

We made it home a few minutes later to find yet more challenges waiting for us. Our local church leader had come round to visit and one of the other lads in the house had made him a cup of tea and was in mid conversation. Pete and I bundled through the door, making a lot of noise, still giggling about his bump with the car. Upon discovering the pastor, Pete headed for his room, but I decided to engage the bewildered man in conversation. How much sense I made I have no idea! After an hour or so our visitor made his apologies and left, and I went to look for Pete. I eventually found him asleep in the garden, having gone outside because he felt sick. His evening was completed by a visit to the owner of the car he had hit to own up to the accident and offer to pay for any damage. Needless to say, we didn't head for the bar in the afternoons again for a little while. We definitely went too far that day.

Food and drink are a huge part of the culture of student life. Most people would think of students not eating well and having more than enough to drink. Of course these ideas in part are true, but they are by no means the full story. Students tend to have a food culture of their own, eating at irrational times and yo-yoing between taking meals out and poor nutrition at home. There are those who are geniuses at rustling up a gourmet meal in a few minutes from simple ingredients, and there are others who struggle to boil an egg. In general, standards of student food are improving, both in catered and self-catered accommodation. Publications aimed at helping students to cook have improved confidence, while the need to prepare students better to fend for themselves is also now more widely recognised. Even churches are helping by offering students lunch on a Sunday and creating schemes where church families can adopt a student to look after by offering them meals as well as support.

Everyone knows that alcohol can be a problem in the student world, but surprisingly little is done to make students aware of the risks of drinking too much or to support them if they find themselves in difficulties. Poor nutrition and alcohol abuse form a powerful cocktail as students are left to fend for themselves. I have known one or two who have had to learn difficult lessons the hard way, often feeling isolated and eventually even leaving uni altogether because they couldn't cope with the issues of eating and drinking they had to face.

Catered and self-catered halls

A lot of students will have some of their nutritional needs looked after for them when they start uni because they will live in a catered hall. The food may not always be that appealing, but it will usually provide a balanced diet, and normally at least two meals will be available to each student every day. Halls are getting better and better at providing a good range of healthy food options, and most students are now more aware than ever of the need to try to vary their diet and choose from a range of food groups. Catered halls are a great option, and for the majority of students it is the best way of making sure that neither they nor their parents have to worry about what they are going to eat. If this option is available I would advise you to take it, unless you are pretty confident in the kitchen. Hall fees that include food can be a little more expensive, but for the convenience and peace of mind it is worth it.

Self-catered halls will provide a good range of kitchen facilities, and you will have your own cupboard space that you should be able to lock. You will have to look after yourself from there on in though, buying and cooking your own food for every meal. This is often where students get into difficulties, as they may have little or no culinary experience and perhaps no strong desire to try obtain it. Stories of students existing purely on jacket potatoes and beans are not rare, and I have known one or two friends who at times have hardly eaten at all because they have not been able to provide for themselves.

If you are in self-catering your budget may be a big factor, as you might be reluctant to spend much on food, preferring to save money for essentials such as books and beer! The supermarket could be quite a distance from your hall, further reducing your chances of getting to a decent shop to stock up the cupboard. Parents are often very good at sending their student offspring back to university with a large box of goodies to keep them going at mealtimes. This can be a massive help, encouraging you to make a good start to the term and saving you the effort and expense of a couple of weeks' shopping.

Students like to get together and share their food with one another. This not only provides a good social occasion but also helps food to go further and looks after those who are not so competent in the kitchen. I know of one or two girls who regularly cook for their whole corridor and are known as 'Mum' to all their mates.

Eating disorders

Students can be susceptible to eating disorders, which

they have often been battling with since their early teenage years. Research done by the Eating Disorders Association (EDA) shows that young women aged between 15 and 25 are most susceptible, although of course men can be affected too. The nature of student life only adds to the anxiety of those who suffer from eating disorders. The pressures to attract others and fend for themselves have in some cases combined to create a problem where before there hasn't been one. These issues are rarely discussed in normal student life, yet numbers of young people with eating disorders are on the increase.

The EDA website explains what eating disorders are and how they may be caused:

> Eating disorders develop as outward signs of inner emotional or psychological distress or problems. They become the way that people cope with difficulties in their life. Eating, or not eating, is used to help block out painful feelings. Without appropriate help and treatment, eating problems may persist throughout life.
>
> Eating disorders are complex illnesses where both the disturbed eating pattern as well as the psychological aspects need to be treated. Restoring a regular eating pattern plus a balanced diet is needed for balanced nutrition. Helping someone come to terms with the underlying emotional issues enables them to cope with difficulties in a way that is not harmful to them.

For more information on specific eating disorders and

their symptoms, have a look at the EDA website at www.edauk.com.

Supermarket sweep

Cooking on a tight budget is never easy, but it can be done. Your money will go further if you stick to products you can buy in large quantities (rice, pasta, cereals, crisps) and avoid expensive luxuries (chocolate, ready-made meals, fruit juices). Buying loads of fruit and vegetables will add to a healthy diet and keep your costs down, as these things are relatively cheap. Meat is expensive, but you can make it go further by adding lots of cheaper vegetables like onions and potatoes to whatever you are cooking. Try to avoid buying lots of unnecessary extras and consider sharing with others things you may all use a little of, like salt and pepper, vinegar and tomato ketchup. Make a list before you go shopping to prevent you from being drawn into buying things you see at the last minute, and choose carefully where you shop and what brands you buy to help keep your costs down. Try to find out where the local market is held, as this is by far the cheapest place to buy fruit, vegetables, eggs and spices. Try not to go shopping when you are hungry, as you are likely to buy half the store!

Eating on campus

On any student campus there will always be plenty of

places to eat. There should be at least a couple of different restaurants to choose from, plus other snack bars and shops where you can grab a sandwich. At some unis they offer a system whereby you can add credit to a card and exchange credits for food at one or two places on campus. This can be handy to avoid having to think about cash, but can work out expensive if you use it regularly. A lot of students will buy food at lunchtime on campus and there are usually some large spaces where crowds will gather to eat and chat. If the bar is not open, you are probably not on a student campus. Most students will eat out fairly frequently as this is an important part of the culture. Student towns are full of cheap places to eat, most of which will offer a discount to students who can show some ID. Curry houses are usually the most popular, and in a student city they will rely on students for most of their custom.

Knowing when to stop

If food is an important part of the life of a student, drink in the form of alcohol is like the blood flowing through their veins. The vast majority of students drink heavily at least once a week and a fair percentage will have a drink most evenings. I remember when some friends and I decided to enrol at the uni gym and were required to give some information to the receptionist before we were allowed on the machines. When asked how many units of alcohol each of us drank my friends lied without exception, saying they drank 10 to 15 units per week. A realistic figure would have been more like 50 units for most of them, which equates to 25 pints of beer or 50 glasses of wine. For one friend's 20th birthday, the group I was part of decided to celebrate by matching his number of years with the number of pints they would drink. One or two of them made it, and I ended up carrying the birthday boy back to his room that night. The social scene and the sports scene at uni are both dominated by alcohol, and as a student you will come up against the issue again and again. How can you engage with this culture without becoming consumed by it and getting sloshed three times a week?

Some Christians would say that you should not drink at all. Others would say that drinking is fine and you shouldn't worry about it, as long as you know when to stop. It is easy to make a sweeping statement like that, but when it comes down to it the pressure to be one of the gang at uni and sink as many pints as you can is enormous. This is not just a problem for the lads either. More and more girls are drinking to excess, often leading to health problems in later life. Research published in November 2001 showed that a high percentage of young women aged between 18 and 25 were drinking far too much each week and that abnormal numbers of women in the same age group were reported to have suffered from severe liver problems. It is no coincidence that this age group accounts for most of the student population. Many of the young women in their early twenties who reported problems were said to have started drinking heavily while they were a student. Alcoholism is also on the increase, particularly among young people, and studies have shown that drinking vast quantities of alcohol as a student can easily lead to alcoholism in a matter of months.

A good friend of mine knew that drinking could be a real problem when he went to uni. He is a normal lad who likes a beer and rarely gets drunk, but he wanted to be careful in the first few weeks of uni, so he decided to stick to soft drinks for the first term. He knows himself well and thought that for him it was better to say he wouldn't drink at all than to risk going too far if he tried to have just a couple of pints. He stuck with his plan all through the first term and decided to keep to it for the rest of the year. He's graduated from uni now and he never did have a drink all the time he was there. Funnily enough, he never got drunk either. I'm not suggesting that this should be the code of conduct for every Christian trying to hold on to their values, but it is a good example of thinking before you act and making a choice which, although it is a sacrifice, will help you live the way you want to. Self-control is one of the fruits of the Spirit listed in Galatians 5 and I can think of no finer example than the choice my friend made before he went to uni.

However much sound advice is given out, sometimes people make a mess of things and get into difficult situations. I know of one or two students who have struggled with eating disorders and a few who have had major problems with alcohol. These things are real and they affect students, perhaps even more than other parts of our society. If you, or someone you know, is having problems with one of these things, there are people who can help you come out the other side. Every uni has a welfare office that provides counsellors to listen to and advise students on these and other issues, and they will assist you in finding more specific help if you need it. There is a list of national initiatives to help with these and other issues at the back of this book. ▶▶ `appendix 1:` `national helplines`

11

sport and health

Playing sport for a hall is usually great fun. Our hall was good at rugby – in fact we were very good. We had several semi-pro players in the team, the type of guys who were able to make the game look easy, hardly breaking into a sweat. Due to a break in the fixture list, and the fact that we were looking for a challenge, we took up the opportunity to play some teams from a local league. They had an odd number of teams in the league and the spare team each week welcomed the chance to play a practice match against us. It was supposed to be friendly. One of these games was against a team whose players all lived in the same area of the city. The area, and consequently the team, was infamous for being mostly made up of men who had been in prison in the last few years.

We arrived to a frosty reception and the game kicked

off with hardly a word spoken between the two teams. Their game plan seemed to be intimidation and they proceeded to go in very hard at every opportunity and to throw a few nasty comments to our players to try and wind us up. We were wary of their attitude but not about to give up the game when we thought we should win.

By half-time we were well ahead in the game and began to relax and enjoy playing. Then the fun started. After half-time they seemed to come out even more aggressive and violent than before the break. Several punches were thrown, players were stamped on, and at one point even the crowd seemed to want to get involved. We managed to endure the onslaught, hoping it would not get any worse, and eventually finished the game winners by a comfortable margin. The strange thing was that as soon as the final whistle was blown the atmosphere lifted and the local team became very friendly towards us. They invited us into the clubhouse for a drink and congratulated us on how well they thought we had played. We declined their kind offer and headed for our team bus, not sure how long their smiles would last. I thought uni sport was competitive, but compared to what we experienced that day, the other games we played that season were nothing!

A lot of students take sport very seriously. At most unis the facilities are excellent and students can take part in a wide range of sports, at any level, for almost no cost. Typically a medium-size uni would have its own swimming pool, athletics track, sports hall, courts for tennis, badminton and squash, a fully equipped gym, and playing fields for all the major team sports. Coaches and instructors are normally provided to help teams improve, although students themselves normally take on the management and organisation of the teams. Each sport will have its own club, again run by students, which gives everyone who wants to the opportunity to learn and play the game of their choice. In the major sports, such as football, rugby, hockey and netball, there will normally be at least two teams that represent the university against other unis, as well as competitions between halls and other friends-based teams that come together informally.

Serious or social?

These are the two sides of university sports. Some of the top teams representing the uni each week against other universities compete at a very high level. Competition for places can be fierce, and players will be expected to be very committed to the team and train hard. For top sportsmen and women, this will become their number one priority and they will spend many hours working to be the best they can. Some of the very best of these people may even represent their country at international competitions. Others will be asked to play for teams that represent towns and cities in the national leagues. Some universities, such as Loughborough, have gained a reputation for being excellent at sport. Some of the courses available for study here are sports-orientated and many of the teams they put out are the best in the country. Other unis have no record to live up to, but enjoy the challenge of competing in the national university leagues. Wherever you study, the range and accessibility of the sports available to you will be impressive.

The social side of university sports is much less serious but no less competitive! Many students play for fun, enjoying the exercise and community that are the benefits of sport. With so many good facilities available, most students have a go at something during their time at uni. While play on the field is of a reasonable standard, it is the off-field antics of these clubs that are legendary. Team sports are normally played on Wednesday afternoons, which are reserved across the country to allow universities to play each other every week. In most cases there will be no lectures after lunchtime on this day, to allow everyone the opportunity to get out and play. The social side of the sports clubs really kicks off once the final whistle has been blown for the afternoon, and the team can either celebrate or commiserate their result together.

It will be no surprise that drinking again plays a prominent role here. Most teams will spend a lot of Wednesday evenings together and experience shows that the majority of players will leave for home having consumed vast amounts of alcohol. Unfortunately, this can also be where team places are won and lost. Initiation ceremonies for uni sports teams are infamous, and often only those who are willing to humiliate themselves and join in with whatever is dished out by the established regulars will find themselves in the starting team for the next match. Drinking games, naked streaks, dares and bets all feature regularly, so if you are going to get involved, be prepared to stand up for yourself and know how far you want to go. The peer pressure in sports teams can be immense and the draw of a place in the top side seems a big prize if you are willing to pay the price. Team culture is powerful, and individuals often encourage each other to be far more daring than they would ever be on their own or away from this environment. I have known a few friends who have played along hoping to make it into the first team and ended up being completely humiliated and with no place to show for it. Be careful! If you are a Christian this can often make you a target for those around you who may see you as a challenge and try that bit harder to get you to do something you would rather not. The other side of the coin is that others have shown it is possible to stay out of trouble and prove yourself on the field.

One friend of mine who was an excellent hockey player was disappointed when she was left out of the first team to represent her uni. She was clearly one of the best players available, but had chosen not to degrade herself in the off-field activities. When she was picked for the third team, she knew that she had been victimised for making a stand. She stuck with it and when, after a few weeks of matches, the first team had struggled to win their games, she was restored to the side and spent the rest of the year as a first choice player. The next year she was asked to be captain and was able to change the culture of the team so that players were always picked on merit. The team still socialised together, but while she was captain a player was never asked to show her skills anywhere but on the field.

As a student you have a great opportunity to try something new. As well as the mainstream sports available in every uni, more unusual sports are available too. You can try almost anything! Extreme sports are very popular and students of all abilities from novice to expert can join a club for relatively little cost compared to what you would expect to pay if joining a private club. You will be surprised at what is available if you check out the stalls at Freshers Fair, or the notice boards that each sports club will have, probably in the Student Union building. These clubs will welcome beginners and more than likely invite you along to try out whatever they do to see if you like it. Membership of these clubs is normally very cheap and all you will need to pay for is the equipment you use and any fees required by external venues. Clubs often organise overnight trips and holidays to allow students to travel further afield and spend more time on their chosen sport. If there is something you have always wanted to try, the chances are you will be able to at uni.

Sport is one of the main things to help keep students healthy at uni. The opportunity to get out into the fresh air and run around for a few hours each week is a great privilege that many working adults would love to have. Of course, non-sporty students can do as they wish, and many who are not involved in a formal club will use this and other times in the week to have a kick around on a spare patch of grass, visit the gym or just catch up on some sleep. Uni can be an assault on the body, and students need to be aware of what they can do to look after themselves. Late nights, a suspect diet and lots of alcohol can combine to make students feel drained and undernourished. Sport and a bit more sleep will help, but in some cases more needs to be done.

Staying healthy

There are three main types of health problem that students face: illness, depression and stress. Each of these can be serious if not dealt with properly.

Illness

All humans suffer from being unwell from time to time, but students are particularly vulnerable because of their lifestyle and the fact that they often live together in very close proximity. Glandular fever, meningitis and flu are by far the most common of the serious illnesses that can affect students. The symptoms for these conditions are very similar, which is part of their danger. Students who have one of these will feel very tired, have bad cold symptoms, feel stiff, possibly sick, and want to stay in bed. Most students showing these symptoms will have flu, but a few may have one of the other two illnesses. The giveaway with glandular fever is that the sides of the neck, the area around the glands, will be swollen. Meningitis sufferers will not be able to tolerate bright lights and might have a rash that does not disappear when pressure is applied. If you suspect that you or a friend has any of these illnesses it is best to get them to a doctor as soon as possible. Severe meningitis can kill within 24 hours and a few students die of the illness every year, so don't hang about if you are worried at all. While flu sufferers will need a few days in bed, anyone who has glandular fever or meningitis will need a good period to recover and will be unable to work, exercise or drink alcohol for some time. All three of these illnesses are passed on by close contact with others, so it is wise to be careful when kissing, using the same cutlery and sharing food with other students. Glandular fever is known informally as the kissing disease because it is passed through saliva and can often spread in a student hall very rapidly!

Depression

The second major health problem faced by students is depression. Approximately a third of people in the UK suffer from some form of depression at some time during their lives. For those who have not suffered from depression before and have not experienced a traumatic event in their lives, it is not uncommon for depression to develop in their early twenties. Students are particularly vulnerable because of their lifestyle and surroundings. Often students feel isolated while they are living away from home and they struggle to adjust to the diminished support and care experienced through this. While students may have a lot of friends, they can often feel as though they do not know the people they live and work with well, and that they cannot share their more intimate thoughts and concerns. Added to this is the fact that many students feel under pressure because of the demands of their coursework and their worries about money. Studentdom is unpredictable and often students feel a lack of control and certainty about their circumstances and sometimes fear what may lie ahead. Doubts, anxiety and a sense of hopelessness can build up, and without adequate support to be able to talk about these feelings students can quickly spiral into depression. Unpredictable sleep patterns, lack of vitamins and minerals, and the darkness of winter can all contribute to making the condition worse.

If you feel you might be suffering from depression, however mild, you should visit the doctor to talk through how you feel and work out how you can get better. With some help and support almost all depression sufferers will start to feel better quite quickly; often simply being given a regular opportunity to talk about how they feel will help to beat this illness.

Stress

The third health problem encountered by students is

stress. Most students will feel pressured by work, money or personal issues at some time during their studies. Often these feelings will pass quickly, but sometimes students can feel so worried about their circumstances that they will become unwell. Loss of sleep is very common, which only makes matters worse. Friends will often begin to notice when a student is suffering badly from stress, as they will become agitated and unsociable, look tired and withdraw from group activities.

If you are stressed about any part of your life, or know someone who is, there are some things you can do to alleviate your feelings. The first thing is to take a break and move away from whatever is worrying you. Go for a walk or a coffee with a friend and share how you feel, so that someone else knows and can support you as you sort it out. If you need help with your work or your finances, be brave and go to see a tutor or a counsellor to talk through the problem. They will be able to give you advice that will help you solve the issue. At some point take time to try and plan how you can recover from the situation, thinking logically about how much time you need to get things straight. Meanwhile you should ask one or two good friends, and perhaps your parents, to support you. Usually these types of problems can be overcome relatively quickly once you resolve to make yourself vulnerable to others and get some advice.

What can you do to help?

Christians are called to care for those around them and particularly to pray for those who are unwell. If you have friends who are ill or suffering in some way, go and see them and offer your support. You can ask them if they would like you to pray for them, and if they will let you, pray with them then and there. Remember to pray for them in the next few days and weeks until they are completely better, and back up your words by helping them in practical ways. You might be able to do some shopping for them, fetch some books from the library, buy them a magazine, or arrange to borrow a TV from a friend. This is one of the best ways that you can show God's love to those you live with and demonstrate how powerful prayer can be. God will honour you when you step out for him and he will not miss the opportunity to work in your friends' lives.

Is any one of you in trouble? He should pray. Is anyone happy? Let him sing songs of praise. Is any one of you sick? He should call the elders of the church to pray over him and anoint him with oil in the name of the Lord. And the prayer offered in faith will make the sick person well; the Lord will raise him up. If he has sinned, he will be forgiven. Therefore confess your sins to each other and pray for each other so that you may be healed. The prayer of a righteous man is powerful and effective. (James 5:13–16)

12

the student union
and societies

The Student Union is the hub of student activity on campus. Every university has one and when you register on campus during your first week as a student you are automatically enrolled in the union. Usually the union will have its own building, which will house the student bar, shop, cafés and loads of other facilities. Events nights will also be held here, with the place being transformed into a nightclub for regular weekly events, and balls each term. Not only does the union organise entertainment for students, it also represents them to the university and across the country through the National Union of Students, or NUS.

Your first contact as a student with the union is likely to be during Freshers Week, when much of the activity of the union will be concerned with showcasing what services it provides and what clubs you can join. A Freshers

169

Fair normally runs for a few days during this week, when a large hall in the union will be filled with stalls, which sports clubs, societies, banks, shops and clubs can use to tell you about what they offer for students. Most students, including non-first-years, will spend a good few hours here to see what is available and to sign up to any clubs they want to join. It's a good idea to have a careful look around before you sign up for anything, as you may find you have to make a choice about what to go for. Societies and sports clubs are desperate for you to sign up and pay a small membership fee, because they want to attract as many students as possible to their activity and may well get additional funding from the union for each member they have on their books. Freshers Fair can be a good place to find out more about a student bank account, or pick up a bargain at one of the stalls selling useful items. There is usually a second-hand bookstall, and often a poster stall providing a cheap way to decorate your new bedroom. You should leave Freshers Fair with a good carrier bag full of free goodies, information and useful bits and pieces. Most stalls use some kind of giveaway gimmick to attract you to visit them in the first place, so you can feel happy in having got something for nothing. ◀◀ 3. starting uni and freshers week

Getting involved in the union

Once Freshers Week has been and gone, the union will

revert to a normal weekly pattern of events to serve the student community. There may well be a market every week that is similar to Freshers Fair, but with more stalls selling useful cheap goods. Other weekly events will include themed club nights, and each of the societies will normally hold their own meeting. The societies make up a good part of the work of the union representing, various social interests of the student body. Most unis will have a few different religious societies, a society for international students, a debating society and societies for some courses. These are student led and run, and a lot of students get involved in at least one society. For those who are committed to their society, this can become their main social meeting point and form a large part of their student life. The union becomes a very interesting place whenever two or more of these societies have a dispute with one another over a particular issue. Christian groups are often involved in this type of dispute as they will debate with other religious groups and sometimes run into trouble with the union itself because of their stance on certain issues. Two common examples are discussions with the Islamic society over the difference between the two religions, and issues with the union over Christianity and homosexuality. I have been involved in both of these debates, both as a student and working alongside Christian students, and have been impressed with how maturely and wisely students deal with these issues. Usually there is not a longstanding problem if everyone involved is willing to show a little tolerance and understanding towards those who think differently from the way they do.

The union is a debating forum for student issues. There is a student council that oversees the running of the union and provides an opportunity for hot issues to be discussed and, if necessary, voted on. This can be a very influential gathering, as its opinions are likely to be listened to by the university authorities, and the union will help to inform the NUS on national policy. The NUS is a representative body for all students in the UK, mainly speaking to the government and media on student issues. In recent years one of the biggest issues the NUS has taken up has been that of student debt, as more and more students have had to increase their borrowing. The NUS has campaigned for the government to increase its funding of higher education to reduce the burden on individual students, who can easily have debts of five figures by the time they graduate.

Sabbatical teams

The Student Union is led through each academic year by a team of former students, usually known as a sabbatical team, or sabs. Each year elections are held to fill these posts and there are usually a few nominations for each role. Typically one person will be president and there will be four or five deputies with responsibility for matters such as finance, entertainment and welfare. This can be a great chance to influence a whole university and to serve a group of students for the year.

The sabs are normally paid a minimal wage and can either take the post at the end of their studies or take a year's break to do the job. It is very normal for a Christian to stand for at least one of the posts in each year's elections. Often all the other Christians will tend to vote for this person, which is not unusual because most people will vote for someone they know. I have often thought that it would be better to vote for the person you believed could best do the job and would best serve all the students of the university in the post. If that person happens to be your friend, then so much the better.

The union gets pretty wild around election time as those standing for the posts campaign to win votes. Usually a few stunts are pulled to attract the punters, and this can make for some good entertainment in between lectures.

Mark Lloyd Davies studied biology and geography at Royal Holloway, University of London. After the final year of his degree, he became President of the Student Union.

'I wanted to "get involved" and contribute to the student community from my first day at Royal Holloway. In my first year I considered standing for the post of First Year Representative, and was eventually persuaded to do so after chatting to the president. From then on various people started encouraging me (and sort of mentored me) to stand for other posts.

In my second year I was elected Constitution Officer, the

most senior position on the executive, as one chairs that meeting and the General Meetings. In my third year I focused on my degree, but made clear my intention that I would run for President in the second-term elections.

The best part of the job was being a Christian there and sharing my faith with the kind of people who would not even contemplate going to a CU evening. The worst part was the continuous integrity battle; sometimes you felt as if you were in two worlds.

Being the President of the SU was extremely hard work, but it was definitely worth the effort. As Vidal Sassoon once said, the only place where success comes before work is the dictionary. My advice to anyone considering getting involved in their SU is this: never underestimate the power of role modelling; be yourself, proclaim your faith and just watch God do the rest – it's as easy as that.'

Important issues

The union is your opportunity to get involved at the heart of student life and make a big difference for your fellow students. Whether you join a society, stand for election or simply join in with one or two debates, this is a place where your voice can be heard. A lot of Christian students find it hard to speak on some of the issues that come up in the union because they don't know what to say and are afraid of what opposition they might meet. To help you get started on some of these hot student issues, here are a few responses for you to think about.

Student debt

Debt is a consequence of the fact that people do not have all they need and have had to borrow from others in order to pay for it. In the case of student debt, it is the Student Loans Company that students owe money to. There are two things to consider here. First, there is the issue of need. Most students believe that they need to have a degree in order to get a better job when they begin work. In the most part this is shown to be true because employers have pushed the benchmark higher for entering certain jobs, and the government has heavily endorsed higher education as the golden standard that all young people should strive for. While I think we should encourage as many people as possible to go to university, it is no coincidence that since the higher education system has been broadened to be more inclusive of different academic abilities, so the financial strain on the system has increased, and students have been forced to fund their own studies, instead of the money coming from a central pot as it used to. Perhaps the government should do more to find ways of training people for employment without them necessarily having to have a degree. Soon a degree will no longer be good enough for some jobs, as greater demands are placed on those wishing to enter certain occupations.

Second, there is the issue of responsibility. Who is responsible for your education? Is it your responsibility, your parents' or the government's? Everyone agrees that it is down to the government to provide basic education for all young people. This is paid for from tax revenue. Some would argue that it is not fair for everyone to pay more tax in order for some to benefit from higher education, and they are probably right. Once you have graduated you are very likely to earn a far higher wage than someone who left school to go straight into the workplace. Perhaps the government could stop the student loan system and simply increase the basic rate of tax for those who have graduated from university and whose earnings are above a certain threshold. This would mean no debt, but those who have benefited from higher education would take responsibility to pay for it.

From a Christian perspective debt is a tricky issue. The Bible says that we should not let a debt remain outstanding (Romans 13:8). If you take that to mean that we should not borrow money, then in today's culture it would be very difficult to buy a house or a car, or to pay for your education! I think a more realistic definition of debt is to think of it as money that you owe and cannot pay back. That is when you need some help to sort out your finances!

Religious freedom

Religious groups at university are often called to account by the union because of their attitudes towards certain practices, which are deemed as prejudice, something the union is unlikely to tolerate. In return, religious groups sometimes feel as though they are being restricted in what they can and can't do by the rules of the union. It is a difficult balance to get right, but I think it is worth making every effort to stay with the union while upholding your core beliefs.

Where this has been difficult to resolve, a number of student groups have disassociated themselves from the union to avoid coming under the regulations. In my opinion this is not the best answer, as being a member group of the SU is an important part of what a Christian group should be trying to be. Where there are differences of opinion – however strongly they are voiced – this is an opportunity to engage in important dialogue with non-believers. Christian groups should be the first to show tolerance and understanding towards other groups, to get to know those of different faiths, and to be an active part of the Student Union. Usually an agreement can be reached which allows Christians to protect their beliefs and a greater degree of friendship and discussion to emerge.

Though I am free and belong to no man, I make myself a slave to everyone, to win as many as possible. To the Jews I became like a Jew, to win the Jews. To those under the law I became like one under the law (though I myself am not under the law), so as to win those under the law. To those not having the law I became like one not having the law (though I am not free from God's law but am under Christ's law), so as to win those not having the law. To the weak I became weak, to win the weak. I have become all things to all men so that by all possible means I might save some. I do all this for the sake of the gospel, that I may share in its blessings. (1 Corinthians 9:19–23)

Homosexuality

This is the one issue Christian student groups get nailed on again and again. Most non-Christians have a perception that Christians are homophobic and preach against homosexuality. This widespread opinion causes Christians to be seen as bigots, and at times causes Christian groups to be accused of prejudice. I have been involved at one university where a Christian group was threatened with expulsion from the union because they were believed to be anti-gay. When we should be the market leaders in accepting people whoever they are, Christianity is again seen from the outside to exclude and reject people. Leviticus 18:22 tells us that God commands that a man should not lie with another man as he would a woman. God finds the act of homosexuality detestable. Most Christians would agree on this. But God finds any form of sexual immorality detestable, as he does stealing, lying and swearing. Hands up anyone who has not done any of those things. The fact is that we are all practising sinners, and very few of us are 100 per cent sexually pure, whether we like girls or boys. Christians need to be a lot more tolerant of gay men and women so that they are not prevented from having a relationship with God. Of course I'm not suggesting that homosexuality goes unchallenged, but together we can all help each other to do less of the things God says we should not do. Making the distinction between those who have homosexual feelings and the act of homosexual sex should help others to understand what it is you believe and enable the group to be more accepting of everyone in the student community. ◄◄ 9. relationships and sexuality

13

holidays and travel

Travelling has become something of a phenomenon in the student community. Increasing numbers of students take the opportunity to see more of the world before, during or after their studies. When I returned from the summer break to start my second year at uni it was hard to believe the stories flying around my hall of what my friends had been up to for the last three months. One guy had been to America to work on a children's camp as a sports coach. Another person had bought an InterRail card and spent two months catching trains around Europe. Someone else had been to South America. One girl I knew had spent most of her summer smuggling Bibles into China! As I listened to all these stories I felt a surge of jealousy rise up in me. I wanted to go to all of those places! Without exception, it seemed my friends had travelled the world for next to nothing, and were intent on going on about it for the rest of the term. What had I been doing all summer? I had worked in a petrol station and built a new patio for my mum and dad. At least I had a suntan, I suppose.

I have been lucky enough to travel a lot since then and see many of the things my friends described that summer, but I remember feeling at the time that somehow I had been left out. I had missed something. I didn't even know that half of those opportunities existed. Being a student gives you the fantastic privilege of having long holidays that can be used in so many different ways. As if that were not enough, if there is something you really want to get your teeth into, you can take a gap year from your studies and spend that time on your chosen activity too. The key to both of these things is to plan well ahead.

Making the most of the holidays, particularly the three-month summer break, is relatively easy if you start thinking about what you want to do in advance. It's important to make sure you know the options available to you. I have listed the main ones here.

Travel

Holidays or a gap year provide adequate time for you to see some of the world for relatively little cost. It is amazing to hear of some of the places students manage to travel to. I have had friends who have been skiing in Alaska, and others who have chosen to spend two months tramping around in the jungle in Brazil. Whether you want to travel for two weeks or two years there are agencies that can help you put your trip together, giving you all the information and advice you will need. One of the best of these, particularly for round-the-world packages, is STA (Student Travel Association). They are specialists in student travel, and their website, www. statravel.com, is packed with ideas and essential information. A lot of students choose to take a year to travel with their friends after they have graduated, knowing that once they have financial commitments they will not have the same freedom to be away for so long. The traveller's path is now well worn and fairly safe, providing you stick to the advice the travel company give you and are careful in certain countries. Most destinations will play host to thousands of foreign travellers at any one time, so you will not be isolated for very long. Comprehensive travel insurance will cover you for any medical needs or anything that gets stolen along the way.

The 1999 film, *The Beach*, has done nothing to dampen the desires of a generation of travel-hungry students. Just like Richard, the main character in the film, many students are 'looking for something more beautiful, something more exciting ... [even] something more dangerous'. Richard certainly found what he was looking for. The beach in the film, which actually exists on an island off the coast of Thailand, is the idyllic dream many travellers are searching for. Alex Garland's novel, on which the film is based, tells of this paradise where time, background and prospects are irrelevant; all that matters is the beauty of the beach and the sanctity of the community who live on it. These sentiments convey something of the truth of what travelling is about: people from all over the world, mixing together and having an adventure, while visiting places they have never been to before and seeing things they have only dreamed of. Many of us have the travelling bug, and I know for sure that every time I watch that film I want to jump on the next plane to Thailand! If you want to travel, there will never be a better time than while you are a student.

Work

You may choose to do some paid work during the holidays to give your finances a much-needed boost. A lot of students will take temporary jobs for a few months during the summer to earn as much as they can for the year ahead. Future travellers will often work before they head to the airport to raise the funds for their trip. Casual jobs for students are plentiful and you should be able to find something quite quickly, but be prepared to work long hours and in rough conditions for a few weeks if you want to maximise your earning potential. Warehouse jobs are very popular, often involving a lot of manual labour. Shops often take students on too, provided you are going to be around for a while, allowing the permanent staff to take holidays while you cover for them. A temping agency will be able to line up an office job for you at short notice, but be advised that this kind of work is usually very dull and badly paid because the agency will take their cut first. If you can find a job you enjoy, which you can return to each holiday, you will have landed a good deal. Alternatively, you could look into taking a working holiday abroad. This may not increase your bank balance as much as stacking the shelves of your local supermarket, but it will broaden your horizons. Check out www.bunac.org for more info on this type of experience.

Placements

If you are likely to want to work in a profession that requires experience and contacts, such as law or accountancy, you may want to consider the option of using your holidays to take a work placement. Although there is a lot of competition for places in the top firms and often placements are unpaid, getting this type of experience can be incredibly valuable. Placements will vary in length from one week to several months, so it is perfectly possible to spend some time on a placement and the rest of the holiday travelling or in a paid job. For some occupations, going on a placement is a must to get ahead of the crowd when it comes to looking for a job after uni. Your course tutors and careers service on campus will have more info on what is available to you.

Claire, a former UEA student, took a placement at the

Gallup Organisation, a leadership consultancy based in
Kingston, Surrey, between the second and third years of
her degree. Here she describes her experience:

*'I found out about the company through a friend and want-
ed to make contact with them because I really believed in
the ethics behind their work and was interested in knowing
more. I emailed them asking them for a short work experience placement. They had never had work experience students before so they asked me to complete an Internet
"strengthsfinder" assessment to see if I was the right type
of person to visit. I was nervous beforehand, as I'd never
experienced a large office environment. However, the
recruitment team I was based with were extremely welcom-
ing and accommodating. Although there were times of simply observing, they found loads of interesting stuff for me to
do. The managing director also gave me some time with her
to discuss my week and my future plans. The fact that they
do extensive research on what makes a successful company
was reflected in the office climate, which was professional
and friendly. I really enjoyed my time there as it gave me a
glimpse of lots of different work areas within a large firm
and helped erase my preconceptions that employees look
down on work experience students.'*

Service

You may want to take some time to serve others during
your holidays. This can often involve travel to another

part of the world, being part of a team and helping others to achieve something they can't do on their own. There are loads of opportunities for service available and a good range of organisations that run schemes you can get involved in. My room-mate at uni took the opportunity one summer to take part in a scheme called Camp America (www.campamerica.co.uk). This is an organisation that runs children's holiday camps in the United States, and recruits students and young adults to be staff members for each camp. To make a successful application you need to have an interest in working with children and some skills to offer the camp, and you will be paid a small wage. Camps run for about eight weeks, after which you are free to travel for a few weeks before returning home. The whole trip can be arranged and paid for by Camp America, so this is a great option to see another part of the world. Be prepared to work hard though!

There are also a lot of Christian organisations that offer opportunities for service during the holidays, usually focusing on mission. Oasis (www.oasistrust.org) and Youth for Christ (www.yfc.co.uk) are among the best, although there are lots of other options, depending on what you want to do and where you feel most comfortable. Service can add a new dimension to your life as a student and has the added bonus of looking great on your CV!

Jonathan, a doctor at St Peter's Hospital, Chertsey, took the opportunity to travel to Brazil while he was studying at Southampton University.

'I went to Brazil in the summer of 1996 with a team from my uni CU. I decided to go after hearing what happened with the team that went the year before and was stirred concerning the situation with the street children. We went for one month with an organisation called World Horizons (www.worldhorizons.org). Part of the time was spent visiting and helping in a halfway house for street children in Sao Paulo, part of the time doing a mini medical project with an Indian tribe in central Brazil, and part of the time at a missionary training school in the mountains, where we had teaching about mission and were involved in some outreach projects. It was an amazing experience, which I think we got far more out of than we were really able to give. Over the time I was there I felt that God really gave me a heart for children, particularly those who are disadvantaged, and my eyes were really opened to the needs of children in general. This spurred me to get involved in children's work on returning to the UK and also to seek to help overseas in the future. Five years on I am still hoping to go back to South America this year to work for six months. Going on short-term mission overseas has really influenced my life and challenged my ambitions and dreams. I would highly recommend going on short-term mission as it opens your eyes to the situation people are in round the world and it's great to see that we are part of a worldwide church that is living and active.'

Taking a break

Holidays can also be a time for studying, catching up with friends and family, or simply taking a rest. However you choose to use this time, it is intended to be a break from the normal routine of uni life. You may work incredibly hard during this break, but you should return to uni refreshed and ready for a new term. When you are thinking about how best to use an approaching holiday, ask yourself this question: what do I need right now? If you need money, you will want to work. If you need a rest, you might want to chill at home and spend some time with your friends. If you need to get away from it all, you can travel. If you need a fresh challenge, think about joining a team to serve, perhaps in another country. There is no right or wrong way to spend your holiday time, so be as creative as possible and try to do as much as you can. You may never have the opportunity again.

If you don't do it now . . .

Taking a year out is becoming an ever more popular option among today's students. If you have progressed through endless years of education from school to university, never stopping to think what it all means, you may feel the need to take a break at some point. The inevitability of a stressful job in a competitive marketplace may be looming and you might want to take some time to see the world before you start your career. For many, life as a student would not be complete without a determined pause at the end of it all to consider what comes next. You can take a gap year before you go to uni, or even between academic years in your studies, but most opt for taking some time once they have grad uated. With the world at your feet, a few quid in your pocket and a trusty companion at your side, you can't go wrong. Or can you?

Loads of students decide to take a year out but never get past first base. Planning is vital if you don't want to end up vegging in front of the TV and doing odd jobs to keep your mum off your back. A gap year will take a lot more preparation than anything you can come up with during your holidays, so you will need to begin getting it together up to twelve months before you intend to start. Essentially the same options are available to you for a year out as for holidays, but any organised scheme or placement you want to be part of will want to check you out a lot more thoroughly before they sign you up. If you intend to be out of the country for most of this year you should think about what you will do when you return. You may be able to line up a job, another course of study or a placement for your return, which will save panicking when you are due home, or endless correspondence while you are away. If you are travelling it could be very difficult to manage an application from the other side of the world.

A lot of year-out options will be excellent preparation for your future. At Joshua Generation we offer a year programme that helps to develop you as an individual, as well as give you some experience in working as part of the team. Seeing a year out as an integral part of your vocational journey is vital if you are not to end up wasting your time and a lot of money. Some Christians feel they *should* give a year of their lives to God before going on to start their career. While this is very noble, I am afraid that the sentiment is misplaced. God does not want a year of your life. He wants all of it. If you believe you can serve God just as well in a bank or as a teacher as you can on a mission team or working for a Christian charity, then why should the whole of your working life not be dedicated to the service of God, whatever field you choose to go into? I'm not saying that spending time working as part of a Christian organisation is not valid. Of course it is, but it does not immunise you from serving God in every hour of every day for the rest of your life. Hopefully when the time comes, you will be able to find a job in which you can do just that. For a Christian that is what work is all about. ▶▶ 16. career and vocation

14

church in student culture

One cold, rainy, winter evening I decided enough was enough. I had avoided the 'church issue' for too long. It was time to go. I hopped on my bike and rode across the city in the general direction of where I knew a church to be. As well as avoiding rushing Sunday motorists, I had to try and work out exactly where this place was. Eventually, after a good 20 minutes of searching and a couple of near-death traffic incidents, I found the run-down building in a cheap part of town. No one welcomed me at the door as I shook the rain off my coat. No one smiled as I entered the back of the chapel. No one spoke to me as I sat alone on the back row of the half-empty church meeting. I can't remember much about the meeting itself. There was no doubt a bit of singing, a few notices and some kind of talk. I left as soon as I could, having spoken to no one at all. I don't think anyone even looked at me. There were no other students there and I never went back. It was a long time before I went to a church meeting again.

What are you looking for?

Most cities fortunate enough to host a university or two will have a few churches that aim to cater for the needs of students. These churches become known as 'student churches'. In any one city there is usually, but not always, a mix of student churches providing for different preferences among Christian students. A few of these churches are exclusive to students, but spending almost all your time with people your own age can be limiting and the majority of students value a sense of family in their church community.

Having said this, there is often a problem of integration. A lot of Christian students attend a church, but far fewer feel as though they are part of the church. It is very easy for students who have been Christians all their lives to go along to a Sunday meeting a few times a month but never really engage with what it means to be part of a church the rest of the week. For those who have come from a close church family, this can come as something of a shock. There are three main problems that cause this to happen again and again.

First, expectations can be a problem. Most students expect to be part of a church that adapts to the rhythms and patterns of student life. Most churches have a wider church family to cater for, from children to pensioners, and cannot tailor their programme solely to the needs and demands of students. Often this results in churches doing little more than hosting a student group and making sure students can get a free lunch on Sundays. While this is a good start, it does not really help students to cope with the unique challenges of student life. I frequently meet students who have struggled to see the relevance of what their church offers them, often resulting in them going to fewer and fewer church meetings, and perhaps eventually losing touch altogether.

Second, timing can be a problem. Most church activities will happen at the weekend when the majority of the population has time away from work or school to meet with their friends. Quite often this can involve a reasonably early meeting on a Sunday morning. For most people this is not a problem; for students it can be a nightmare. Weekends and weekdays do not have the same distinction for students as they do for everyone else. Although there will be no lectures, students do not work a five-day week and don't tend to plan their spare time around weekends in the same way that most of us do. Sometimes as a student it is difficult to tell what day of the week it is. In addition to this, Sunday morning is not the best time for students to meet with the rest of their church. Students spend a lot of weekends away from uni, visiting friends or returning home to spend time with their families. A lot of internal sports matches are played on Sunday mornings, and students often stay out partying very late on a Saturday night, making it very difficult to attend a morning meeting the next day! A lot of churches hold a meeting on a Sunday evening, which goes some way to helping with this issue.

Third, understanding can be a problem. Church, when understood as a meeting that you attend on a Sunday, does little to help students live from Monday to Saturday. You cannot just *go* to church. The apostle Paul spent a considerable amount of time explaining to the people of Corinth, in first-century Greece, that they *were* the church: 'Now you are the body of Christ, and each one of you is a part of it' (1 Corinthians 12:27). In the same way, you are the church, every minute of every day, whether you are in the company of other Christians or not. Understanding this can help us make a tremendous breakthrough in addressing the question of student church. If you are the church, the question you should ask yourself is not 'Which church shall I go to?' but 'How shall I express church in my student culture?' The church exists to glorify Jesus and to tell others who he is. Therefore as a student you, along with your Christian friends on campus, are charged with the same responsibility. It is essential that students interact with other parts of the body, as they can support, pray for and disciple them to achieve this goal, but they should not be restricted to fitting into a style of church that suits those who are not students. Those churches that resource and support students best are those that understand this and help their students to glorify Jesus and reach their friends on campus. This may take a few adjustments!

Breaking the mould

Finding a way of being church as a student is a challenge, both for students themselves and for the churches that seek to help them. In many cases it is the city churches that must take seriously their responsibility to support students and help them to express church for themselves in their culture. Sometimes students will need to be pushed to do this, as by far the easier and more established approach to student church is one in which the church outside of student culture takes the lead and creates a programme that students can come to in order for their needs to be met. When this happens student culture itself is not touched by Jesus through the church, as the church remains distinct from student culture. Only when students living as the church, and being empowered to do so, express church in student culture, will God radically touch those students outside the church. Something actually has to happen in the everyday lives of students for this to be outworked, and the church should see the university campus as part of its mission-field through the lives of its student members. The responsibility for winning students to Christ does not rest on students or on the Christian groups on campus alone, but also on the church whose city that university is part of. What then can you expect of a student church?

1. *A church that lives to glorify Jesus and tell others about him.* This goes without saying for any church, but it is

worth taking some time to get to know people in the church, finding out what their vision is and how they are going about it. If you want to be part of a church that is committed to being the best it can be, you will want to make sure it lives up to your expectations.

2. *A church that has a vision for students.* It is essential that you are part of a community that understands what life as a student is like. Your church should be active in tailoring some of its resources, teaching and discipleship to the needs of students and should be strongly motivated towards reaching and winning as many students for Jesus as possible.

3. *A church that adapts to the student lifestyle.* Caring for Christian students and helping them to reach their friends with the gospel are tasks that place unique demands on a church community. You should look to be part of a church that is willing to break with some of its cultural traditions for your benefit and to empower you to be the church every hour of your life.

4. *A church that meets students' needs.* It's essential to get involved in a church that teaches the Bible faithfully and in a way that is relevant to student life. You should look for somewhere that helps you learn from Scripture and provides pastoral care to help you live what you learn.

5. *A church that encourages student leadership.* The best people to help students glorify Jesus and introduce their friends to him are students themselves. A stu-

dent church should nurture students to be leaders in the church and on their campus. As in any culture, student churches will need the guidance and experience of those of older years, but students should be able to express themselves as church in their own culture.

6. *A church that will invest in your future.* University is a preparatory school for the rest of your life. Your time at uni is not just about being part of a cool church and seeing some of your mates get saved. It is also a major opportunity to get clued up on how you are going to live the rest of your life and to get some time with one or two people who can mentor you.

No church is perfect and very few will be able to deliver all the above at once. Being part of church is more about making a contribution than finding out what you can get from everyone else. Paul reminds us in the same letter to the Corinthians that everyone has their part to play in making up the body. Whatever your talents, you can offer everybody else something of yourself to enrich their lives, lead them closer to Jesus and help them share their faith with their mates. Put simply, that is what church is all about.

Ness Wilson is the leader of a church in Loughborough (Open Heaven) that has sought to encourage students to express church in their culture. He comments:

'The purpose of the church is to be a relevant and accessible expression of church for students (and increasingly graduates as more and more are staying on with us!). We are now made up of current students (about half the congregation), graduates from the last few years and a few who have joined us from outside of Loughborough – about 125 in total. A typical week would consist of cells happening midweek that are the main meetings of church life and then a Sunday evening gathering. We don't tend to have loads of extra church programmes as we want Open Heaven to be dispersed and active among the halls, clubs, societies and workplaces.

'Students are our priority and determine when and where we meet on a Sunday. There's also the fact that student culture is reflected in all we do – we have refused to get slick and professional – and that students are taken seriously and given real responsibility within leadership roles. Students are not an "add on"; they are the core group that we reach out to and build with. We have high expectations of what can happen in a student's three years' studying – we see maturity way beyond people's years because they are the leaders and decision-makers within our community.

'We try to support students in their everyday lives through one-to-one discipleship. We encourage everyone in the community to be discipled by someone and disciple someone else. It works out that many of the current students are being discipled by recent graduates, who can help them through the various challenges of student life. We obviously provide teaching and discipleship material on all

the common areas of student pressures. Our influence on campus is mainly through individuals rather than us as an "organisation".

'We let the students know they have a blank piece of paper upon which to invent church in their culture – they do not need to copy anything else they've seen. A first step to expressing church in student culture is student cells on campus, which embody all the essential qualities of what it is to be church, e.g. community, growth, discipleship and outreach. The next step could be student-relevant events or gatherings – ideally on campus and organised by the students themselves. Finally, a student congregation could be released, which would have a student leadership team and be empowered to carry out all the normal functions of church life, e.g. baptising new believers, breaking bread, preaching, teaching and equipping the members to be active and involved in campus life, making a difference at every level.'

Pete, a member of Open Heaven, has described the church as being a great support in helping him live as a Christian student, and a source of continuity when he and his wife decided to stay in Loughborough after they had graduated. I know that Pete has been discipled by the leaders of the church and that being a part of the community with his student mates was a large part of their decision to live in the town after uni.

For many Christian students, the extent to which they engage with the church during their time at uni can make or break their Christian journey. Make sure you get integrated with a church community that can help make your student days a time of major growth in your relationship with Jesus and equip you for the rest of your life.

15

christianity on campus

I f there were anywhere on earth I would like to live apart from in Great Britain, it would be America. There is something about the extravagant culture of the United States that attracts me. Of course it has nothing to do with the food or the weather! I have been lucky enough to visit the States quite a few times in recent years and was particularly pleased a little while ago to be able to spend some time with American students in a number of universities. As the schedule for my trip was coming together, I was intrigued to notice that one of the places my American friends had arranged for me to visit was Texas Christian University. I spent longer than usual preparing what I wanted to say to the students at TCU on that day because I was sure they would be spot-on with their theology and would expect me to give a presentation of the highest standard. After all, a university with the word 'Christian' in its title can only mean one thing, right? It must be full of Christians.

Wrong. TCU was not full of Christians – in fact there was only a very small group of Christians on campus, who went to great lengths to tell me that the rest of the university was about as far removed from the basics of the Christian faith as it was possible to be. As we walked around the campus my hosts pointed out to me a landmark that I later found out was the source of some debate among the student fraternity. On the cornerstone of the main building of the university was an inscription declaring that the college was built to glorify God. Literally, one of the cornerstones of that university was the Christian faith. Apparently for the last few years there has been a growing campaign among the students to have the stone removed and to change the name of the university. It seems TCU would rather be known simply as TU.

You do not have to travel to the United States to find a university that was established by Christians to glorify God, and which has since turned its back on that heritage. The University of Westminster in London has a mosaic in the middle of the floor of the entrance lobby to the Students Union that bears the inscription 'The Lord is our strength'. That college too was established for a higher purpose, but sadly there is little reflection of those words in the life of the university today, though the university chaplain is very proud of their floor!

Thankfully, although you may be able to take the word 'Christian' out of the name of a university, remove a cornerstone from its structure or deny its heritage of faith, you cannot get away from the fact that there are thousands of Christians studying in our universities today. Christians have been meeting on university campuses in the UK for hundreds of years, and the culture of student life has always been one that has encouraged Christian students to think for themselves and grow in their faith. The unique environment that life as a student creates is a test for the sturdiest of faiths, but one which if successfully overcome can make for a committed, radical and passionate disciple of Jesus.

Everyday living

As a Christian student, you can expect a lot of this growth to take place in your everyday life, particularly through your relationships with your friends and the wider community that life as a student provides. There is a myth among Christians that your faith is developed in church meetings, when you are reading a Christian book, or when you attend a conference. Of course all of these things are helpful, and they will be able to give you encouragement and support to live the life, but it is in the ordinary rhythms of life that you will mature the most. Jesus rarely asked his disciples to come out of the everyday context of life in first-century Palestine, but was careful to make sure that the group lived among the people they intended to serve and learned the lessons he had to teach them as they went along.

As we have seen in the previous chapter about church, there is a lot that non-students can do to help and support students in their life at university. The empowerment of the local church is vital as students unravel what it means to be the church in their unique culture. Advice and care from home can also make a lot of difference, particularly for new students as they settle into student life. In addition to all this, there is the vital role that Christian student groups play in supporting students throughout university life and resourcing them to reach their friends with the gospel. There are a number of student ministries that aim to cater for the needs of Christian students during their time at university.

The Christian Union

The Christian Union (CU) movement was established in 1928 and has a strong heritage of supporting Christian students. Almost every university and college has a CU, which aims to gather together all Christian students on campus and resource them for student life. At the top of the agenda for CUs are two vital components in the life of Christian students: mission and maturity. CUs consistently encourage students to share the gospel with their friends, often providing innovative tools such as student-friendly booklets that have been specifically designed for distribution to non-Christian students. They also encourage students to grow in their relationship with God and find a balance between their faith and student culture.

CUs usually hold a weekly meeting, often somewhere

on campus, where students can worship together and a speaker is invited to give some teaching to the group. These meetings will often involve prayer for current issues and notices of what the group is doing in the coming weeks. CUs also tend to run small groups in halls and residential areas that aim to give more time to building friendships between Christians, studying and discussing the Bible, and encouraging each other to share the gospel with friends. Occasionally, CUs will hold a mission week of evangelistic events, and often run special meetings for international students and Freshers at the beginning of the year.

The University and Colleges Christian Fellowship (UCCF) is the national network of CUs. It provides a team of staff working alongside the students who lead each CU, to support them and train them to fulfil the CU vision effectively. They hold a national conference in September each year and regional training weekends. You should look to get involved in the CU at your university if you want to get to know lots of other Christians, grow in your Christian faith and be inspired to share the gospel with your friends.

Fusion

Fusion was established in the mid-1990s and is a network of church-connected student cells (small groups) around the UK. Fusion seeks to support and resource students who want to meet together in cells to share their lives, pray and reach their friends with the gospel.

Fusion has grown rapidly as many students have embraced the value of being part of a church community that is looking to engage with and reach student culture. Although cells normally meet weekly, the emphasis is not on cell meetings but on interaction between Christian students and the impact their lives can make on their student friends. The cell philosophy is based on a principle of growth and multiplication, so Fusion cells should be looking to add their friends to the group, see them come to faith for themselves and then have the cell multiply as it becomes too large to be one group.

Fusion runs a national conference for cell leaders each year and provides cell notes and other resources to support cells as they grow and multiply. They are continuing to build a network of churches that support their work and will connect with student cells as they emerge. In a few cases CUs have replaced their small groups with Fusion cells and attempted to blend their activities together, with varying degrees of success. You should join or start a Fusion cell if you want support from a local church-based group to live as a Christian student and see your friends come to know Jesus.

Navigators

Navigator groups, commonly known as Navs, focus on the discipleship of Christian students. The Navigators has a strong tradition of evangelistic work and is particularly known for its work with new Christians. There are currently twelve universities across the UK that have a

Navigators group, often in association with the CU, meeting weekly for teaching, discussion, prayer and worship. These groups are supported by a national student ministry that runs conferences and provides resources to support Christian students. You should get involved with a Navigators group if you are looking to find out more about sharing the Christian faith.

Agapé/CSA

Agapé, sometimes known as Christian Student Action (CSA), is an evangelistic ministry that seeks to encourage Christian students to reach their friends with the gospel. It focuses on training students in evangelism and equipping them with resources that will help them lead their friends to Christ. Agapé/CSA groups can be found on quite a few campuses, particularly in major cities, and often work in connection with the CU or other Christian groups. Often students will be members of Agapé/CSA and another student group on campus. Agapé/CSA runs national training initiatives and conferences, and has teams and individual workers available to assist students in mission. You should get involved with an Agapé/CSA group if you are serious about evangelism and want to see as many students as possible reached with the gospel.

Alpha

Alpha for Students is part of the international Alpha initiative based at Holy Trinity Brompton in London. The

Alpha course is a practical introduction to the Christian faith designed for non-churchgoers and new Christians. The Alpha for Students team supports student groups and churches running the Alpha course in their university and provides training and materials to equip them. In addition they host a conference each year for course leaders and run regional days around the UK when you can get together with other people involved in student ministry in your area for training and interaction. Alpha is purely an evangelistic tool and not designed to provide for other students' needs. It can therefore be used by any group or combination of groups on campus. You should get involved in running Alpha if you want to share your faith in a non-threatening low-key environment.

Christians in Sport

Christians in Sport (CIS) is a national initiative that seeks to encourage sporty people in their Christian faith and inspire them to use sport to share the gospel with their friends. Many universities have a Christians in Sport group, normally made up of members of other Christian groups on campus whose main interest is sport. CIS runs a national conference each year and provides support and resources for each group. CIS also supports men and women who are at the top of their sport and often runs events where well-known sports personalities share their faith. You should join or start a Christians in Sport group if sport is one of your main interests and you want to be able to share your faith with your friends through sport.

SPEAK

SPEAK is a team of people whose aim is to make students aware of justice issues and to help them to pray and campaign about these concerns. SPEAK is growing fast as students catch on to its passion and hear more about justice issues around the world. It holds a national conference each year and has a small team available to visit universities and share what it is doing.

SPEAK groups are springing up in many universities, gathering together students who feel strongly about justice and who want to campaign to see situations changed. SPEAK also provides resources to help students understand, engage with and pray for the issues it raises. You should start or join a SPEAK group if you are concerned about justice and you want to know how to do something about it.

Joshua Generation

In my work with Joshua Generation, I have had the privilege of getting to know many people who work with or are a part of the above-mentioned groups. Their contribution to the lives of many Christian students has been immense. Joshua Generation is a team that invests in emerging generations of leaders, to transform society. Part of this work is focused on preparing students for their future, by helping them to make the most of the unique opportunity university provides to get ready for what comes next. JoshGen does not have groups on any campus but works alongside other student organisations and churches to equip students for the rest of their lives, often specialising in vocational training.

As well as these national initiatives there are a number of smaller agencies that work with students on a regional level, or national movements that gather students at a conference or stream. In addition, every university has a chaplaincy, whose staff are mostly ministers from denominational church traditions such as Anglican, Baptist, Catholic and Methodist. The chaplaincy exists to provide for the spiritual needs of all students on campus and often has a valuable ministry in helping and advising students who are not connected to any other Christian group and even those who have no Christian faith. It is common for chaplaincies to support denominational societies, where students from particular Christian denominations can meet together and worship in a style more particular to their tradition. Often these students are members of other Christian groups on campus and in most places the relationships between Christians from different groups are good. Unity events and joint prayer meetings are common, where Christians come together to encourage and support one other as they follow Christ and witness to their fellow students.

An integrated life

It is fantastic that there are so many groups you can plug

into while you are a student. One danger of having so many things happening on campus is that it is possible to get a lot of Christian input but miss out on the benefits of being part of a church. Too often campus groups are detached from the work and influence of local churches, and students can feel torn between their church and being part of a group at university. To overcome this I would encourage you to find ways in which you can bring the culture of your church onto your campus, and vice versa. It is essential that campus groups are seen as part of the body of Christ and that they relate well to the rest of the body in the town. Churches need to take seriously the role they are called to play in supporting Christian students and sharing the gospel in universities. Equally, student groups need to be in close relationship with churches in their university city and attempt to see the activity of their group as part of the work of the body there. It can be tempting to try and separate out what is church and what is a student group, but in fact it is more healthy to allow the boundaries and distinctions to become blurred in order that church and student life can flow in and out of one another, and the culture of the university can be penetrated with the kingdom of God, which is God's culture carried by the church. ◀◀ 14. church in student culture

You may find, as you become part of a Christian group on campus and a local church, that a lot of people spend almost all of their time with Christians. When I was at uni there was one guy who used to stand up in a CU meeting at least once a month and berate the rest of the group for living in a 'Christian ghetto'. The sad thing is that he was largely right. It is so essential for you, as a Christian student, to have a blend of friendships, and particularly to work on your relationships with non-Christians. Sometimes it can be really hard to stick it out with a crowd of your mates who are living in a way that tests your boundaries, but it is worth hanging in there, loving them and winning them for Jesus. God loves students so much and he wants to be able to show them that love and be introduced to them by you. It's always so much easier to meet someone when you are introduced by a mutual friend.

When Jesus started his three years of ministry on earth he was baptised in the Jordan, tempted in the desert for 40 days and then returned home and began to speak about what was going to happen:

He went to Nazareth, where he had been brought up, and on the Sabbath day he went into the synagogue, as was his custom. And he stood up to read. The scroll of the prophet Isaiah was handed to him. Unrolling it, he found the place where it is written: 'The Spirit of the Lord is on me, because he has anointed me to preach good news to the poor. He has sent me to proclaim freedom for the prisoners and recovery of sight for the blind, to release the oppressed, to proclaim the year of the Lord's favour.'

Then he rolled up the scroll, gave it back to the attendant and sat down. The eyes of everyone in the synagogue were fastened on him, and he began by saying to them, 'Today this scripture is fulfilled in your hearing.'

All spoke well of him and were amazed at the gracious words that came from his lips. 'Isn't this Joseph's son?' they asked. (Luke 4:16–22)

As Jesus read these words, the crowds in the synagogue stood and watched, amazed. These are some of the most powerful words in Scripture, and here was the carpenter's son reading them to his home town. As if that wasn't enough, when he finished reading the passage, he put down the scroll and said in effect to everyone listening, 'This stuff is about me. I'm going to do this. And it starts right now.' They must have been gobsmacked. The point is that Jesus was right – he had come to do all that the Scripture said he would, and he has been doing it ever since. He is the one! In John's account of Jesus' life, Jesus set us a challenge, saying:

I tell you the truth, anyone who has faith in me will do what I have been doing. He will do even greater things than these, because I am going to the Father. And I will do whatever you ask in my name, so that the Son may bring glory to the Father. You may ask me for anything in my name, and I will do it.

If you love me, you will obey what I command. And I will ask the Father, and he will give you another Counsellor to be with you for ever – the Spirit of truth. The world cannot accept him, because it neither sees him nor knows him. But

you know him, for he lives with you and will be in you.
(John 14:12–17)

Jesus not only said that he had come to do all those
amazing things himself, he also promised that if you follow him you will do them too. In fact, you will go one
step further! This is an amazing challenge to Christians
around the world, but in the last few years I have come
to realise that nowhere is it more relevant than on our
university campuses.

Many of your student friends are blind and are
oppressed by the culture of the world they live in. They
have no more ambition than to get drunk, sleep with
someone they have never met, graduate and land a job
that will earn them shed loads of money. If you are not a
Christian there would seem to be nothing wrong with
those things, but if you are, you know how much more
a relationship with Jesus can deliver. The great thing is
that as you try to live as Jesus has shown you, and tell
people what life is all about, you are not on your own.
God has sent the Spirit to be with you and live in you.
You don't have to save the world in your own power;
you just have to be a friend to the person next to you,
trusting God to work through what you say and the way
you live. In many ways that is what all the Christian
groups on campus exist for: to help you walk with Jesus
and show your friends the way to heaven.

So here's what I want you to do, God helping you: Take your everyday, ordinary life – your sleeping, eating, going-to-work, and walking-around life – and place it before God as an offering. Embracing what God does for you is the best thing you can do for him. (Romans 12:1 *The Message*)

16

career and vocation

At a nativity play last Christmas one little girl who took part, aged about four, ran to her mum as soon as her ordeal was over. 'Mum, Mum,' she said, 'I want to be a nurse!' Mum looked down, picked up her child and asked what had brought on this sudden vocational urge. 'Well,' said the little girl, 'I don't want to be a shepherd!'

Knowing what you want to do when you finish university is not easy. A lot of students still have no idea what comes next when they are handed their certificate on graduation day. For those who have done a vocational course, like medicine or law, the choice is of course a little easier. However, for most students, finding a job in which they feel happy and confident is a challenge. Very few people look forward to the prospect of work, but for most students there is a great sense of excitement about discovering what the next part of their life will hold. Making the decisions needed to get there can prove a lot more taxing. After a few weeks of searching through job ads and talking to careers advisers, it can feel as though it might be easier not to bother.

Why work at all?

In the light of God's creation and the mandate he has given us to look after the earth, work makes perfect sense.

> Then God said, 'Let us make man in our image, in our like-ness, and let them rule over the fish of the sea and the birds of the air, over the livestock, over all the earth, and over all the creatures that move along the ground.'
>
> So God created man in his own image, in the image of God he created him; male and female he created them.
>
> God blessed them and said to them, 'Be fruitful and increase in number; fill the earth and subdue it. Rule over the fish of the sea and the birds of the air and over every liv-ing creature that moves on the ground.'
>
> Then God said, 'I give you every seed-bearing plant on the face of the whole earth and every tree that has fruit with seed in it. They will be yours for food. And to all the beasts of the earth and all the birds of the air and all the creatures that move on the ground – everything that has the breath of life in it – I give every green plant for food.' And it was so.
>
> God saw all that he had made, and it was very good. (Genèsis 1:26–31a)

God worked to create the earth and continues to work to sustain it. We are made in his image and therefore are created to work as he does. Before the fall of Adam and Eve, work was not what it is now. Work was always meant to be a challenge, to stretch our minds and exercise our bodies, but it was designed to be enjoyable, an integral piece of our partnership with God. Sin has made work painful and human beings lazy.

> To Adam he said, 'Because you listened to your wife and ate from the tree about which I commanded you, "You must not eat of it," cursed is the ground because of you; through painful toil you will eat of it all the days of your life. It will produce thorns and thistles for you, and you will eat the plants of the field. By the sweat of your brow you will eat your food until you return to the ground, since from it you were taken; for dust you are and to dust you will return.' (Genesis 3:17–19)

Thankfully, God did not leave us to it after the incident in the Garden of Eden, but he has continued to encourage us to work and to make a difference. For our benefit he has given guidelines on how we should work (Exodus 20:9–10) and declared that work is his gift: 'Moreover, when God gives any man wealth and possessions, and enables him to enjoy them, to accept his lot and be happy in his work – this is a gift of God (Ecclesiastes 5:19).

The writings of Paul in the New Testament tell us that not only has God created us for work, but he has also prepared work for us to do: 'For we are God's workmanship, created in Christ Jesus to do good works, which God prepared in advance for us to do' (Ephesians 2:10).

Your work is valuable

This is no coincidence. God created the universe and everything in it, including us. He has made us for a purpose: to worship him. This is not just about the singing of songs and being on our best behaviour. It is about the way we live the whole of our lives. Worship is expressed by our relationships with him and each other, how we choose to spend our leisure time and what we do when we are working. He wants it all. I don't believe for a second that this means God wants us to give up being teachers, doctors, bankers and lawyers to be employed by the church. You *are* the church and whatever work you do is of immense value to God and a significant contribution to his kingdom. It is a mistake to feel as though your service for God is somehow umbilically attached to a role within a church meeting or project. Your primary service for God is in whatever work you do throughout each week. This is where you will spend most of your time and where you can serve him best. To understand this is to understand what Paul wrote about in his letter to the Corinthians.

Now the body is not made up of one part but of many. If the foot should say, 'Because I am not a hand, I do not belong to the body,' it would not for that reason cease to be part of the body. And if the ear should say, 'Because I am not an eye, I do not belong to the body,' it would not for that reason cease to be part of the body. If the whole body were an eye, where would the sense of hearing be? If the whole body were an ear, where would the sense of smell be? But in fact God has arranged the parts in the body, every one of them, just as he wanted them to be. If they were all one part, where would the body be? As it is, there are many parts, but one body. (1 Corinthians 12:14–20)

The Oxford English Dictionary describes work as '. . . the application of effort to a purpose, employment or occupation, a means of earning an income'. Frankly, if that's all it is I am not interested. That is where the phrase 'It's just a job' comes from – a means of earning an income; working to pay the bills. There is no sense of enjoyment or fulfilment in that definition. That is why I believe you should not get a job. A job is not what God is calling you to. You should get a vocation. The OED defines a vocation as 'a strong feeling of fitness for a particular career or occupation'. Now that's more like it. That sounds like a way in which you could serve God. Actually, if you read on a little in that definition there is a sneaky addition to the end of the paragraph. It says in brackets 'in religious contexts regarded as a divine call'.

You have a choice

I believe that your vocation is a godly blend of who God made you to be and the work he is calling you to do for him. I am not saying that there is only one job out there for you. If that were the case and someone else had a great interview you could be in the wrong place for a long time. When God put Adam and Eve into the Garden of Eden he said that they were free to eat from any tree except one. Since that time God has always given us free choice in similar decisions, while making sure there are a few boundaries to keep us safe. I do believe that God gives us a choice as to what work we do, in the same way that he lets us choose who we marry. A vocation is a calling to work in a particular field, or even to use a particular set of skills, regardless of what your job title may be.

I have a friend called Fi who knows she is called to be a nurse. She says that she could work in any hospital in the world and she would be doing what God has asked her to do. It is her skills as a nurse that count, not which ward she is working on. A big buzz phrase in the workplace at the moment is 'transferable skills'. These are the skills an individual may have which can be applied to a variety of tasks. Another friend, Jon, is excellent at making decisions, formulating strategies and making things happen. He is a bit of a go-getter. He could work in a lot of different areas of business like marketing, property, communications or retail, but the important thing is that he is using what God has given him to make a difference, whatever field he works in.

Discovering your vocation is a journey without an ending. You will always continue to develop through learning new skills, meeting new people and applying yourself to new tasks. That journey can start right here by thinking about some important questions as you dream of what life after uni holds for you.

What do you want to do?

God made you and he has lined up work that you can do to serve him. He has made not only your skills and talents but also your desires. He has made you to enjoy doing certain things. Those preferences are part of who he created you to be and they can have a lot of influence on your decisions about your vocation. You should look for a job that you will enjoy; something that will stretch you beyond your current capacity and give you satisfaction. That could be almost anything. As long as it's ethical and legal, go for it! Enjoying your work is part of how you worship God through your vocation.

What are you good at?

You are unique. You are very good at some things and not so hot at others. Knowing your personal strengths will help you to know what kinds of job you may be really good at. Your uni course may give you some strong indicators as to the type of profession you will excel in, as will the opinions of your friends. You should look to play to your strengths and find a job where you will be able to perform well, because that is how you were made. There are a number of personality indicator tests available which can help you think about what your particular strengths are. Among the best of these is Strengthfinders, which has been developed by the Gallup Organisation. You can take this test for yourself by buying their book entitled *Now Discover Your Strengths.*

What opportunities are available to you?

As you think about what your vocation may be, take some time to consider what opportunities are available to you and where you may be able to make a contribution. Some options may require extensive retraining, so you might have to cross those off your list. For example, if you want to be a doctor and you have not taken biology or chemistry A-levels and are not currently studying for a medicine degree, you are a good seven years away from achieving that goal. That's not to say it can't be done, but perhaps other doors are more obviously being held open for you.

The story of how my wife, Claire, came to do her current job is remarkable. She had only applied for one job in the months leading up to finishing university. A lot of other people applied for the job too and Claire felt fortunate to be given an interview. She did not have any experience, as this was her first job, and her field of study did not directly relate to the role she was applying for. After the first interview, the panel invited Claire and three others to return for a second interview, disclosing that now they were looking for two people to take jobs with their company. They also told Claire that they were concerned she did not have enough experience and was too young for the role. After the second interview they offered her the job and told her that they were going to re-advertise the other post as they had not found anyone else suitable. Claire knew several of the other candidates, who were all older, more experienced and, on paper, more capable than she was. God gave her that job and she is very good at it.

What has God said?

Often young men and women have had dreams of being in a certain occupation from when they were very young. I know of a guy called Johnny who one day when he was walking to school saw a policeman walking down the other side of the street. From that day on, Johnny knew he wanted to be a policeman and he is now an inspector in the Metropolitan Police Force. Perhaps someone has come up to you out of the blue and suggested you would be excellent in a certain occupation. Could that be God nudging you?

Sometimes the story of someone else who has achieved something in his or her career might inspire you to look into a particular job. As well as through circumstances and friends, God can of course speak in the quietness – what is sometimes called 'the still, small voice'. As you pray and ask God to speak into your vocational decisions, listen to what he has to say to you about

what he would have you do for him in the coming years.
Determining what God has said to you, and whether or
not a thought or piece of advice came from him, is never
easy, but take comfort from the fact that God can bless
you in a number of different jobs and it will soon become
clear if it is not the right job for you.

Work is not easy. It was never meant to be. Each job
brings its own blend of achievements and challenges.
Some days you will be able to finish your work, satisfied
that you have done well. At other times you may feel
restless and stressed as the pressure and complexity of
your working situation tugs at your leisure time. If there
are a lot of difficult choices to make as a Christian at university, there are just as many as a working adult. The
final chapter of this book will give you some idea of the
differences between studentdom and working life.

▶▶ 17. graduation and transition

If you would like to read more about how your faith
can be outworked in your vocation I can fully recommend a booklet by Matt Bird called *Exploring your
Vocation* to be published by Joshua Generation in 2002.
It is a collection of true stories about people who have
found God in their work. The booklet also provides five
steps to discovering your vocation and material to be
used in small groups to help you think about how you
can find a vocation in which you can serve God.

17

graduation and transition

I remember my first day at work as though it were yesterday. I had to commute on a short train journey to our office in Wimbledon. Getting out of bed when it was barely light caused me to register that something new was about to happen. That day was busy: trying to remember where everything was kept, learning how things were done and getting to know my new colleagues was a lot to handle in a few short hours, and before I knew it the day was over. After about 20 minutes at the station, I managed to work out which train I should catch to get home, and eventually walked through the door of my new lodgings feeling as though I had just run the London marathon. I settled down in front of the TV to watch my favourite Aussie soap, forgetting that it had been on about two hours ago, and within a few minutes I was asleep on the sofa.

I just couldn't believe how tired I was. Even though I had prepared well by going to bed early the night before, I was worn out, and it was only the first day of the week. I still had to make myself something to eat and sort out one or two things for the next day before I could eventually go to bed that evening. After a few days of this punishing schedule, commonly known as working life, I began to get used to the change in rhythm and settle into the routine that would be mine for many years to come. As I drifted into unconsciousness that first evening on the sofa, there was only one thing occupying my dreams: my past life as a student.

Any change in life means we have to adapt to new circumstances, become friends with new people and work out what the new rules are. Most people will happily admit they find change a challenge. Not that you won't be ready for it. The vast majority of students I have known have indicated towards the end of their time at uni that they are looking forward to what comes next. When I left uni I moved to a new area and into a new home. I changed churches and had to make new friends. I started a new job and had to cope with a different lifestyle. Pretty much everything in my life was transformed in one way or another during that time, and it was a rollercoaster ride. You may not need to go through as many changes as I did as soon as you graduate, but sooner or later you are going to go through some major transitions as you emerge from the chrysalis of studentdom. Where uni has been a time of preparation, a place to learn and grow, life on the outside is a reality. You will finally have the chance to put it all to the test.

It has to end some time

Graduation is one of the most unique and surreal experiences you are likely to go through in your life. Most people only do it once, and with family and friends gathered to witness your achievement it is a very special day. The time around graduation day can be a bit hectic. For a few weeks after your final exams have finished life will be a mixture of furious partying and nervous waiting for your results to be published. Few people enjoy results day until they have found out how they have done. The experience can be fairly traumatic, depending on how the results are delivered. All unis are different, but on my course the results were pinned to a board at a certain time on the day in question and there was a crush to find out how everyone had done. Not only had we the joy or sorrow of our own achievement, but we were also treated to the intimacy of knowing everybody else's as well. Once results had been collected, almost everyone headed for the uni bar, either to celebrate or to drown their sorrows. For some this was the highest of high moments; for others it was a day they would rather forget. Either way it was the end of an era. Not all students will receive their results in quite the way I did. Some departments prefer to give students a discreet envelope, others post results and some obtain their results by telephone because they are not able to be on campus when the time comes.

By the time graduation itself comes around the frenzy of results day is forgotten. This is a day to get dressed up. You will need to preorder hire of the special gown and mortarboard that graduates are required to wear. Be prepared that this is very expensive and you will feel a bit silly when you put it on, but it is one of the things that make the day unique. You should be able to invite a couple of people to witness the ceremony, and it is worth asking for more tickets if you have someone else who would like to come. Graduation ceremonies can be quite long and involve a lot of waiting around. There will be one or two speeches by university authorities, followed by the main part of the ceremony where each graduand walks across the front of the stage to be greeted by one of the heads of the uni and given their graduation certificate. This could be a little boring if it were not for the fact that this is your big day and all your mates are receiving their degrees too. If you do feel as though the ceremony is dragging on, spare a thought for the vice-chancellor (or whoever is at the front), who may have to sit through three or more days of ceremonies in which he says and does pretty much the same thing. You only have to endure it for an hour or so!

The graduation ball usually takes place in the same week as the ceremonies. This is the most extravagant party in the entire uni calendar and is a must in your last year. Tickets are a bit pricey, but it is almost always worth it when you are enjoying the last party uni has to offer. There is always loads going on at a grad ball, from great bands and DJs to visiting celebrities, fairground rides and novelty entertainers. You will not be bored and everyone will be there to celebrate your time together at uni. Often groups of friends will get together hours before the ball starts to have a meal or drinks and reminisce about their time at uni. Make sure you take your camera, as there will be a few moments you will not want to forget.

What can you take with you?

Graduating from uni is not just a chance to have a big party and celebrate getting a degree. It means a whole lot more than that. It is important to recognise that it is the end of one thing and the beginning of something else. There is a lot you can take with you from your time at uni that will last you a lifetime. You will have made friends who will be important people in your life for a long time after the last dance at the grad ball has ended. You will have picked up skills, knowledge and experience that will serve you well in the years to come, whether they were gained through your academic course or more informally through the maturing journey of student life.

Perhaps you will have been through a dramatic change during your time at uni. Have you become a Christian, chosen a career or decided to get married in the last few years? These things will of course have a

lasting impact too. It is worth sitting down for a few minutes and thinking about what you can take from studentdom as you walk through the door marked 'Exit' for
the last time. Some of the things you choose to pick up
may slip through your fingers in your first few months
after graduation, but a lot of others will last you for life.
Don't underestimate how much of an impact uni has
had on you. You have become more of who you really
are and life will never be the same again.

You have almost certainly changed and developed as
you have lived as a student, and that does not end when
you pick up your degree. You are about to enter another intense period of learning and discovery which will
prepare you for the next few years and act as a bridge
between the world you are about to leave and the one
whose gates you stand before now. Although most graduates will start their career, there are other options you
can explore if you choose.

Some graduates know there is more to learn, and
decide to continue their studies as a postgraduate. With
a bachelor's degree under your belt you can apply for a
place on a master's course or even step up to the challenge of a PhD. Both of these qualifications are a natural
extension of academic study and both require a lot of
motivation and thoughts about funding. Postgraduate
study can be expensive, as the government underwrites
none of the course fees, so you are responsible for everything. Sometimes you can apply for funding from a
grant-making trust or bursary that has a special interest

in providing financially for postgrad students, but such funds are hard to come by and oversubscribed. A master's degree would typically be a one- or two-year extension to your previous field of study, some of which might be taught modules. A PhD will take three years or more to complete and is largely a research project into a new area of study. This is the highest category of academic study available to you, so you must be serious and well suited to research to take it on.

As well as these academic qualifications you can also look into what professional qualifications are available to you which may further your career. In some fields such as law and accountancy further qualifications are almost mandatory, but there are also an increasing number of business qualifications on offer that could get you ahead of the crowd for the job of your dreams. More information on these courses is available from libraries, on the Internet and from business schools direct.

For those who are not quite ready to dive into further study or the world of work, there is of course the option to take some time to travel. This can be a rich experience filled with the sights, sounds, tastes and smells of other cultures, and more graduates each year are taking the opportunity to see the world. It may well be that this is the best time for you to travel while other commitments (partner, children, house, job) are at a minimum and you can indulge in the benefits a round-the-world trip can offer. Travelling will take time to plan and pay for, so make sure you are well prepared and consider working

for a while before you go to raise the cash for your trip.
◀◀ 13. holidays and travel

Going to work

If you do not choose to take one of these options it is more than likely that the workplace awaits you. The transition between university and life as a young working adult is not as straightforward as you might think. A lot of people seem to lose their way along this journey, many saying that they felt pressured, lonely, tired, desperate or used because of the nature of the changes in their life and their new job. For a while now there have been statistics floating around in Christian circles which claim that a large number of solid Christian students have lost their faith during the first few years of life after uni. My experience has shown these stats to be true, as I have seen friends question their foundations and some walk away altogether. It seems that no matter how stable and committed you think you are now, there are dangers that lie ahead which could shake you up and leave you feeling empty and alone. Caution then must be a priority as you head into the workplace for the first time.

A friend of mine describes his transition like this:

'When you are at uni it's like being removed from normal life for three or more years, like in the Armed Forces. When you return to life as a civilian there are lots of adjustments to

make and a lot more responsibilities to face. Life on civi-street is very different from the removed life of a student. I actually thought my gap year prepared me more for uni than uni prepared me for life after uni.'

This kind of experience is very common, as students often don't realise the extent to which they are cocooned while they are studying. As a graduate, the reality of life can come as a sudden shock. One of the key reasons why life after uni can seem so hard is because the large community that student life naturally provides is suddenly removed and graduates can feel as though they are alone in facing new challenges. Often, leaving university will involve moving away from an established friendship group and having to cope with feelings of isolation as well as the demands of a new job. Settling into a new church and finding out-of-work activities can help you to make new friends and give you the beginnings of a new support network you will need to navigate the journey of adult life.

Taking responsibility

Another component of life as a graduate that can take some time to get used to is responsibility. When you become a student, you experience a new level of freedom and autonomy that is not possible as a child living in your parents' home. Although you must look after yourself, this brings with it the chance to make all your own decisions and exercise complete freedom in terms of your lifestyle and behaviour. When you graduate and begin a new job, this freedom is curbed because you face new responsibilities at home and in your work. Your new boss is unlikely to let you start work when you feel like it, nor is he or she going to react well when you have not completed a piece of work when it is required. You will be working to someone else's standards now; the days of setting your own pace are firmly behind you in the corridors of studentdom. Paying your rent, doing your laundry and fixing your own meals all adds to the fun.

Not poor anymore

Finally there is the issue of money. One of the biggest advantages of beginning work is that you get paid for what you do. Most graduate jobs come with a decent salary, and if you only have yourself to look after you are unlikely to be broke. But money brings yet more responsibility as you have to balance necessary outgoings (rent, bills, food, car, student loan repayments) with the desires that having some cash in your pocket is likely to bring out. Never underestimate the materialist beast that can lie dormant within you while you scrape through university, only to emerge hungrier than ever when your bank balance acknowledges the presence of your salary. He will chew you up and spit you out quicker than you can say, 'I've always wanted a DVD player.' Take it easy in the first few months and work out just how much you can afford to play with after all the essentials are paid for. Better to err on the side of caution than over-spend and add to your debts. If you have an overdraft from your student days, get that paid off first. Try to remember what it was like to be poor, and stick to some of the guidelines you had when you were a student, as they will help you stay in the black. Make sure you remember to account for taxes and national insurance, and consider giving a little of what you have to those who need it most.

For more in-depth advice and inspiration on life as a young adult, I can recommend a book by my friend Matt Bird. He emailed loads of his friends in this age group and asked them about the biggest issues they faced. The book is a response to the nine major factors that came back in those emails. It's called *Manifesto for Life,* published by Hodder & Stoughton and is available from all Christian bookshops. Check it out – you will not be disappointed.

Life as a young adult can be even better than life as a student. You can blend the best bits of student life (friends, freedom, self-discovery and independence) with the maturity and confidence that life after uni brings with it. Of course there are challenges and you will have bad days, but you can leave studentdom with the assurance that life will present you with a host of amazing opportunities, and you are ready to tackle each and every one of them.

I have seen the burden God has laid on men. He has made everything beautiful in its time. He has also set eternity in the hearts of men; yet they cannot fathom what God has done from beginning to end. I know that there is nothing better for men than to be happy and do good while they live. That everyone may eat and drink, and find satisfaction in all his toil – this is the gift of God. I know that everything God does will endure for ever; nothing can be added to it and nothing taken from it. (Ecclesiastes 3:10–14)

national helplines

Alcoholics Anonymous: 0845 769 7555
Drinkline: 0800 917 8282
Eating Disorders Association: 01603 621414
National Drugs Helpline: 0800 776600
National Debtline: 0808 808 4000
The Samaritans: 0845 790 9090

national student organisations

Agapé UK (CSA)
Fairgate House
Kings Road
Tyseley
Birmingham B11 2AA
Tel: 0121 765 4404
Email: info@agape.org.uk
Web: www.agape.org.uk

Alpha for Students
Holy Trinity Brompton
Brompton Road
London SW7 1JA
Tel: 020 7581 8255
Email: alpha.office@htb.org.uk
Web: www.alpha.org.uk/students

Christians in Sport
PO Box 93
Oxford OX2 7YP
Tel: 01865 311211
Email: info@christiansinsport.org.uk
Web: www.christiansinsport.org.uk

Fusion
PO Box 58
Chichester PO19 2UD
Tel: 01243 531898
Email: admin@fusion.uk.com
Web: www.fusion.uk.com

The Navigators
Adyar House
32 Carlton Crescent
Southampton SO15 2EW
Tel: 023 8022 3743
Email: info@navigators.co.uk
Web: www.navigators.co.uk

SPEAK
The Shop
487 Liverpool Road
London N7 8PG
Tel: 020 7609 1744
Email: speak@speak.org.uk
Web: www.speak.org.uk

UCCF
38 De Montfort Street
Leicester LE1 7GP
Tel: 0116 255 1700
Email: email@uccf.org.uk
Web: www.uccf.org.uk

joshua generation

Joshua Generation invests in emerging generations of leaders to transform society through mentoring, training and resourcing. In the student scene, Joshua Generation is known for equipping students for their future, particularly through leadership training, vocational preparation and biblical teaching on lifestyle issues.

Joshua Generation
The Church Worple Road
Wimbledon
London SW19 4JZ
Tel: 020 8947 1313
Email: admin@joshgen.org
Web: www.joshgen.org

index

The Unquenchable Worshipper

by Matt Redman

This book is about a kind of worshipper:

Unquenchable. Undivided. Unpredictable.

On a quest to bring glory and pleasure to God, these worshippers will not allow themselves to be distracted or defeated:

Unstoppable. Undignified. Undone.

Worshippers who long for their hearts, lives and songs to be the kind of offerings God is looking for.

'This is unashamedly a book about God and living a devoted life in His presence. Worship is *about* God, *to* God and *for* God. *The Unquenchable Worshipper* shouts this truth out loud.'

Mike Pilavachi, Soul Survivor

survivor

Ignite

by Nigel James

God is setting a new generation alight. They are ready to:

I include Jesus in their moral life, their thoughts, words, actions and relationships.

G grow closer to Jesus through studying the Bible, praying and allowing the Holy Spirit to lead them every day.

N network with other Christians in their country and throughout the world.

I involve themselves in a local church and respect its leadership.

T take the message of Jesus into their school, college or place of work.

E explore God's will for themselves and their generation and seek to follow it.

If you want to be a part of this, this book is for you.

survivor